THE ROMAN WORLD
FROM REPUBLIC TO EMPIRE

Peter Mantin
Head of History, Littlehampton Community School

Richard Pulley
Head of History, Bishop Luffa School, Chichester

CAMBRIDGE
UNIVERSITY PRESS

PUBLISHED BY THE PRESS SYNDICATE OF THE UNIVERSITY OF CAMBRIDGE
The Pitt Building, Trumpington Street, Cambridge CB2 1RP, United Kingdom

CAMBRIDGE UNIVERSITY PRESS
The Edinburgh Building, Cambridge CB2 2RU, United Kingdom
40 West 20th Street, New York, NY 10011-4211, USA
10 Stamford Road, Oakleigh, Melbourne 3166, Australia

First published 1992
Reprinted 1997

Printed in the United Kingdom at the University Press, Cambridge

A catalogue record for this book is available from the British Library

ISBN 0 521 40608 0 paperback

Text illustrations by Chris Etheridge, Peter Kent,
Julian Page, Chris Ryley and Sue Shields

Maps by Lorraine Harrison

Picture research by Callie Kendall

Notice to teachers

Many of the sources used in this textbook have
been adapted or abridged from the original.

Acknowledgements

5*t*, Cambridge Schools Classics Project; 5*b*, 15, 22, 43, Mansell
Collection; 10, 20 *inset*, 38–9, 41, 52–3, 54, 58– 9, 76, Ancient Art &
Architecture Collection; 12, James Morwood; 19, 24 courtesy of the
Ermine Street Guard/photo: Ian Hepburn; 20, courtesy of the Ermine
Street Guard; 27, 45, 63*t*, 65, 70, 71, reproduced courtesy of the
Trustees of the British Museum; 28, Museo e Gallerie Nazionali di
Capodimonte/Bridgeman Art Library; 31, Monumenti, Musei e Gallerie
Pontificie; 37, Photo Library International; 46-7, Gallerie Borghese/
Scala; 49*t*, A. Hopkins; 52, Museo della Civiltá Romana, Rome/Scala;
55, Louvre/© Photo R.M.N.; 58*l*, Christina Gascoigne/Robert Harding
Picture Library; 63*c*, National Museum of Wales; 63 (*house*), Tick
Ahearn; 63*b*, Winchester Museums Service Collection; 67, Aerofilms
Ltd; 77, Cambridge University Collection, copyright reserved.

CONTENTS

POMPEII –
A MOMENT IN TIME

In the year AD 79 a volcano erupted near a small Italian town called Pompeii. Hot ash rained down from the sky, killing many of the people and completely burying the town. Nearly 1,700 years later, the town was rediscovered. Much of what we know about the Romans comes from findings there.

What can we learn about Roman life from Pompeii?

A fatal encounter

On the day of the eruption a man called Pliny sailed to the volcano, Vesuvius. He made the fatal mistake of landing near the volcano to help a friend and to get a closer look.

SOURCE A

Pliny's nephew was nearby and later wrote down the story.

> 'He went to rest in a house near the shore. Soon ash was piling up outside the door, making it difficult to get out. People could not decide whether to stay indoors or make a run for it.
>
> My uncle tried to escape. Although it was daytime it was darker than it is at night. When my uncle reached the sea he found that it was too wild to set sail. The air was thick with flames as a great fire moved towards them. He stood leaning on two slaves and then suddenly he fell down dead, choked by the fumes.'

Letters of the younger Pliny, first century AD

In the town of Pompeii many people died in the same way as Pliny. Fiery ash continued to pour from the volcano until the buildings and bodies could no longer be seen. Pompeii remained buried from sight for many hundreds of years.

Rediscovering Pompeii

In 1748, a farmer digging in the fields rediscovered the lost Roman town. Since then, archaeologists have dug up much of the volcanic ash to reveal Pompeii as it was in its dying moments. About 2,000 people who were killed during the eruption have been discovered. Pompeii probably had a population of around 20,000, with lots of shops, bars, temples and two theatres.

Italy in AD 79, the year that Vesuvius erupted.

4

Source B

The ruins of Pompeii today. The volcano Vesuvius is in the background. This is a view of a road junction in Pompeii. Notice the cobbled surface. The large stepping stones in the foreground were probably for pedestrians to avoid the rubbish that collected in the street.

Source C

The town also had an amphitheatre (arena) where people could watch men called gladiators fight each other, and fight wild animals. This advert was found on a wall.

'Forty gladiators belonging to the priest, Decimus, and twenty gladiators belonging to his son, will fight at Pompeii 8–12 April. There will also be wild beast combats. The seats for spectators will be covered.'

Inscription from Pompeii, first century AD

Source D

These rules were found on the wall of a dining room in the house of a rich man.

'A slave must wash and dry the feet of the guests. Guests should not make eyes at the wife of another man. They should not be rude, get angry or swear. If you cannot keep these rules, go home.'

Inscription from Pompeii, first century AD

By looking at these examples from Pompeii, you may have some ideas of what Roman life was like. As you study the rest of this book you will be able to investigate further the mixture of brilliant achievements and great brutality that made up the Roman world.

Source E

A victim of Vesuvius – a girl who suffocated to death . When the lava from the volcano cooled, it solidified around everything that had been unable to escape. Over the centuries many of these objects decayed, leaving hollows in the solid lava. Archaeologists refilled these with plaster. The lava was chipped away, leaving a plaster cast of the trapped body .

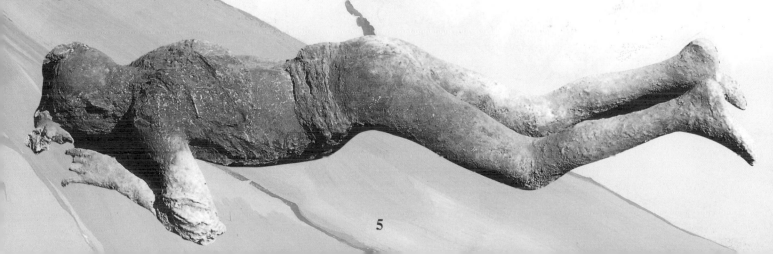

I THE EXPANSION OF ROME

The first Romans were simple farmers. Their territory was no more than Rome itself and the farmland in the immediate area. Throughout Italy there were many tribes, and the farmers of Rome did not seem at all special. Gradually the Romans increased their lands. By AD 117, the Romans had conquered one of the largest empires the world has ever seen.

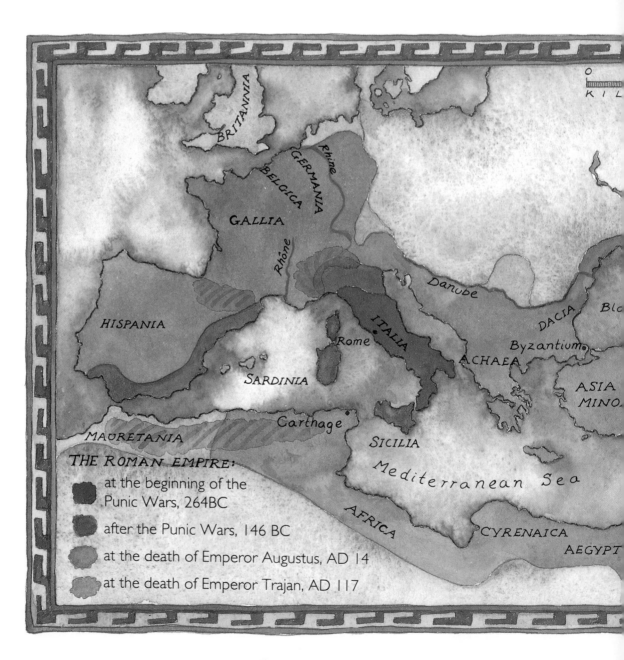

BRITANNIA

GERMANIA
BELGICA
GALLIA
Rhine
Rhône

Danube

DACIA

HISPANIA

ITALIA
Rome

Byzantium

ACHAEA

ASIA MINO

SARDINIA

Carthage

SICILIA

Mediterranean Sea

MAURETANIA

AFRICA

CYRENAICA

AEGYPT

THE ROMAN EMPIRE:
- at the beginning of the Punic Wars, 264BC
- after the Punic Wars, 146 BC
- at the death of Emperor Augustus, AD 14
- at the death of Emperor Trajan, AD 117

1 The map has been divided up into four stages or periods of time.
a During which period was most land conquered?
b During which period was least land conquered?
c Which is the longest period?
d Why do you think historians divide up time into periods?

2 Look at the boundaries of the Roman Empire at the four stages. Make a list of the main physical boundaries of the Empire (rivers, seas and mountains). Do you think physical features were an obstacle, or useful to the Romans?

3 The Mediterranean Sea was called 'Our Sea' by the Romans. Why do you think this was? Can you guess why the sea was so important to the Romans?

4 Can you work out the names of some of the modern countries that were once part of this huge empire?
♦ Hispania
♦ Italia
♦ Aegyptus
♦ Germania
♦ Britannia

The expansion of Rome, 264 BC to AD 117.

ROME AT

I
753 BC

ACCORDING TO LEGEND, ROME WAS FOUNDED BY ROMULUS. THE FIRST ROMANS WERE PROBABLY FARMERS WHO LIVED IN AN AREA CALLED LATIUM.

II
280 BC–201 BC

THE ROMANS HAD CONQUERED MOST OF ITALY. ROME WAS A REPUBLIC WITH A STRONG ARMY. THE ROMANS DEFEATED THEIR DEADLY RIVALS IN NORTH AFRICA, THE CARTHAGINIANS. THEY NOW CONTROLLED THE MEDITERRANEAN SEA.

III
46 BC

THE GREAT GENERAL, JULIUS CAESAR, MADE HIMSELF MASTER OF ROME. THE REPUBLIC COLLAPSED. CAESAR WAS STABBED TO DEATH BY HIS ENEMIES ON THE IDES OF MARCH IN 44 BC.

IV
31 BC

AUGUSTUS CAME TO POWER. ROME BECAME AN EMPIRE, AND AUGUSTUS THE FIRST EMPEROR.

A GLANCE

V
AD 312

EMPEROR CONSTANTINE BECAME A CHRISTIAN. IN AD 313 HE MADE CHRISTIANITY THE OFFICIAL RELIGION OF THE ROMAN EMPIRE.

VI
AD 395

THE VAST ROMAN EMPIRE BROKE INTO TWO SEPARATE PIECES. THE EASTERN HALF WAS RULED FROM CONSTANTINOPLE, ORIGINALLY CALLED BYZANTIUM. THE WESTERN HALF WAS RULED FROM ROME.

VII
AD 410–476

BARBARIAN TRIBES FROM GERMANY OVER-RAN MUCH OF THE EMPIRE, AND RANSACKED THE CITY OF ROME. THE LAST ROMAN EMPEROR OF THE WEST WAS FORCED TO RETIRE IN AD 476. THE WESTERN EMPIRE FINALLY COLLAPSED.

VIII
AD 1453

THE EASTERN EMPIRE CONTINUED FOR MANY CENTURIES AFTER THE WESTERN EMPIRE. EVENTUALLY IT FELL TO THE OTTOMAN TURKS IN THE FIFTEENTH CENTURY.

II THE RISE OF THE REPUBLIC

Between 800 BC and 200 BC the Romans changed from being a small tribe of farmers to being a powerful republic.

How was Rome ruled in its earliest days? How did this change?

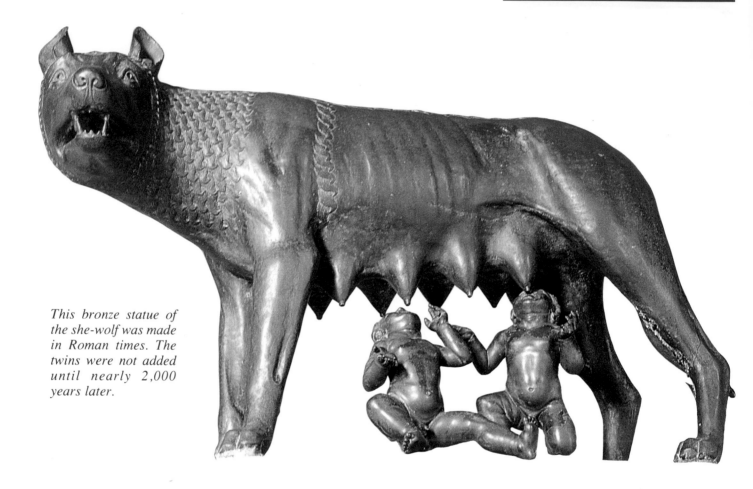

This bronze statue of the she-wolf was made in Roman times. The twins were not added until nearly 2,000 years later.

The legend of Romulus

According to Roman legend, Rome was founded by Romulus in 753 BC. He and his twin brother Remus were sons of the god Mars. When they were babies, Romulus and Remus were abandoned in a cradle on the River Tiber – on the orders of a wicked and jealous king. He did not want the baby boys to grow up and take the throne from him.

The twins were saved when the cradle was washed ashore, and they were suckled by a kindly she-wolf. Then a shepherd found them and brought them up as his own sons.

Later, Romulus and Remus founded a new city on the banks of the River Tiber, on the same spot where they were rescued. Romulus is said to have killed his brother in a quarrel about the new city. Romulus then made himself the king, and called the new city Rome.

Who were the first Romans?

The story of Romulus is a legend. Some parts of the story were made up centuries later, other parts may be true. How can we find out the truth about the origins of Rome?

Archaeologists have found parts of peasant huts on one of the hills of Rome. They think that the first Romans were probably peasant farmers. These people were from an area in Italy called Latium. The language they spoke was Latin.

They began to trade with their neighbours. As Rome grew bigger, a market-place, or forum, was needed for the farmers to meet, talk and trade. The Romans fought regularly against people from the nearby tribes like the Etruscans. Much of the fighting took place in the late summer and autumn, after the crops had been gathered in.

How was early Rome ruled?

Early Rome was a monarchy. This means that it was ruled by one person, a monarch (a king). He was expected to listen to the advice of a council called the Senate. Roman kings were chosen by the senators. The king had a lot of power, so it was important to pick a good leader. He could beat or kill people if he chose to do so. A symbol of his power was a bundle of rods called *fasces* tied together with a red strap. It was carried in front of him by his officials.

● Find out what modern word comes from the word *fasces*. What does it mean?

The Republic is set up

Some kings were good but others were very unpopular. In 509 BC the Romans were so fed up with the harsh rule of King Tarquin that they drove him out of Rome. Some people think that the Roman Republic began when Tarquin was forced to leave Rome. A republic is a country without a monarch.

Roman crests and inscriptions often included fasces and the letters 'S.P.Q.R.' You can find out what this means on the next page.

A man carrying a fasces.

The consuls

The Romans were determined from now on to stop one person from having too much power. Instead of a king, they now had two people, called consuls. To make absolutely sure they did not become too powerful, they were elected for only one year. The job of consul was the most important job in the government.

The Senate

The consuls ruled for such a short time that they had to listen to the advice of the Senate. The Senate was a council of very experienced politicians. Politicians did not get paid, so they were usually rich men. The Senate became much more important in the Republic than it was before. The government of Rome was described by these Latin words: *Senatus Populus-Que Romanus* (SPQR for short). This means 'The Senate and the People of Rome'. You can see the letters SPQR on Roman coins and on the standards carried into battle by soldiers of Rome.

● The Latin word *senex* means 'an old man'. How do you think the Senate got its name?

The citizens

The people who were allowed to vote were called citizens. There were two distinct classes of citizens in Rome. The richer class of citizens were called the Patricians (noble people). They were very wealthy and owned large estates or farms.

The poorer citizens were called Plebeians (common people). They were mostly peasant farmers, merchants and craftsmen. Lots of people were not allowed to vote at all – such as women, slaves and many of the poorest workers.

Even in Rome today, on every drain cover, and on every bus in the city, there is the Latin inscription 'S. P. Q. R.'

Roman society

Some people in Roman times lived in great luxury, while others were very poor. We have looked at how Rome was ruled. How was Roman society organised?

The diagram below shows some of the main groups or classes of people who lived in Rome. At the top of society were the senators. They were very wealthy. At the bottom of society were slaves. They did not have any freedom, and they were not allowed to vote.

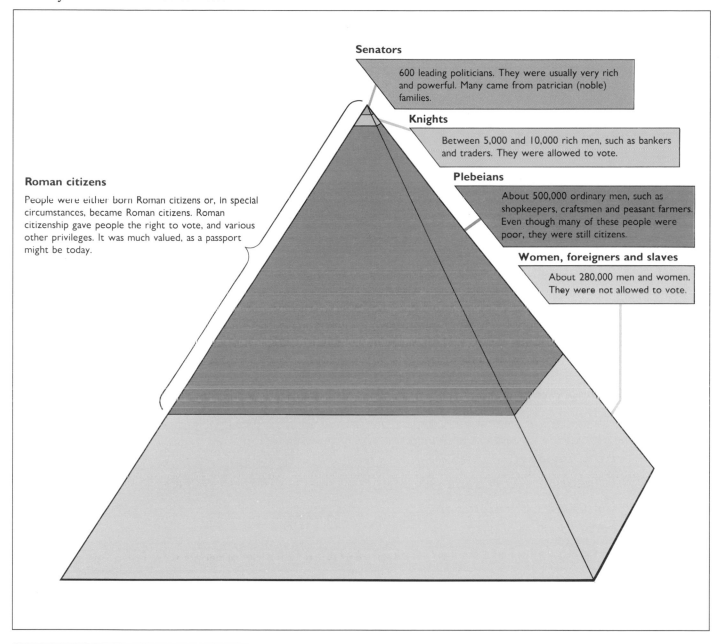

Senators
600 leading politicians. They were usually very rich and powerful. Many came from patrician (noble) families.

Knights
Between 5,000 and 10,000 rich men, such as bankers and traders. They were allowed to vote.

Plebeians
About 500,000 ordinary men, such as shopkeepers, craftsmen and peasant farmers. Even though many of these people were poor, they were still citizens.

Women, foreigners and slaves
About 280,000 men and women. They were not allowed to vote.

Roman citizens
People were either born Roman citizens or, in special circumstances, became Roman citizens. Roman citizenship gave people the right to vote, and various other privileges. It was much valued, as a passport might be today.

---

1 'Rome changed from being a monarchy to being a republic'. Explain in your own words what this means.

2 Here is a list of different groups in the Roman republic.

a Explain who they were.
b Say whether or not you think they were powerful.

SLAVES   CONSULS   SENATE
       PATRICIANS   WOMEN   PLEBEIANS

13

THE PUNIC WARS

In the third century BC, the Romans fought their most deadly enemies, the Carthaginians. The wars lasted over a hundred years. The Romans finally won. This was a great milestone in the setting up of the Roman Empire.

How did the Romans win?

GAUL

Rhône

ALPS

PO

SPAIN

ITALY

Rome

Cannae 216BC

SARDINIA

Carthage

SICILY

Zama 202BC

AFRICA

- land under Roman control
- land under Carthaginian control
- the march of Hannibal
- Scipio's invasion

0   250   500
KILOMETRES

The Mediterranean region in the third century BC.

The struggle for the Mediterranean

By 270 BC Rome had won control of most of Italy. The Romans' main problem was the city of Carthage in North Africa. The Carthaginians were brilliant sailors and their powerful navy dominated much of the Mediterranean Sea. The two powers clashed as Carthage threatened Rome's trade.

Rome and Carthage went to war in 264 BC. This was the first of three clashes which are known as the Punic Wars. The wars did not finish until 146 BC, over a hundred years after the first outbreak of fighting.

During the First Punic War, Rome and Carthage were evenly matched. It took over twenty years for the Romans to win. The two sides made peace in 241 BC. Carthage lost some land and money but remained powerful.

Disaster for Rome

Rome faced even worse problems during the Second Punic War (218–201 BC). A Carthaginian army led by the great general Hannibal invaded Italy in 218 BC. He organised an enormous march for the Carthaginian army from Spain to Italy. He took more than 30 war elephants and about 60,000 men over the Alps. More than half of the men, and almost all of the elephants, were killed, or died of starvation on the long journey.

Hannibal reorganised his troops and defeated the Romans three times in battles in Italy. At the Battle of Cannae in 216 BC, about 70,000 Romans were killed. This was the worst defeat in the history of Rome. The Carthaginians reached the gates of Rome but the Romans refused to give in.

SOURCE A

The peace treaty of 202 BC shows how the Romans were determined not to be bothered by Carthage again.

'Carthage must give up:
100 hostages
all Roman prisoners
all land except a small area around the city
all except 10 warships
all war elephants
200 pieces of silver every year for 50 years
Carthage must never go to war without Roman permission.'

Treaty of 202 BC

Scipio v. Hannibal

Hannibal's army was not strong enough to capture the city of Rome, but the Carthaginians spent many years terrorising other parts of Italy. Eventually the Romans found a brilliant leader of their own. His name was Scipio. Hannibal was forced to retreat to Africa where he was defeated by Scipio in the Battle of Zama in 202 BC.

Carthage must be destroyed

Some Romans were not happy with the peace treaty. They said that Carthage should be completely wiped out. A senator called Cato ended every speech he made with the words 'Carthage must be destroyed'. Carthage continued to be a rich trading state and this annoyed many Romans. After many years the Romans decided to remove their rivals once and for all. In the Third Punic War (149–146 BC), Carthage city was besieged and captured. The town was totally destroyed, the stones were removed and the ground ploughed up. North Africa became another province of Rome. Never again would Carthage be a threat to Rome.

Deadly enemies . . .

SOURCE B
The Roman general, Scipio. A bust probably made in the first century BC.

SOURCE C
The Carthaginian general, Hannibal. A bust probably made in the first century BC.

15

There is only one detailed written account of the Punic Wars that survives today. It is a history book written by a writer called Polybius. Polybius was himself a Greek, but he seems to have done some careful research.

The Carthaginians had been skilful sailors for many centuries. The Romans were not used to sailing. However, during the First Punic War, the Romans decided that they would have to build a navy.

1 'When the Romans saw that the war was dragging on they began for the first time to build ships. The craftsmen had no experience of building large warships, for none of the Italians used such ships, and it caused great difficulty. However, they carried on, and using a wrecked Carthaginian ship as a model, the Romans built their fleet and put to sea. All this shows how determined and daring the Romans are.'

2 'When it comes to fighting on land the Romans are much better than the Carthaginians. The Romans take their army very seriously, unlike the Carthaginians. The Roman soldiers often fight better because they are Roman citizens, while the Carthaginian troops are foreigners and mercenaries, who fight for money.'

The Roman way of fighting is shown in this description of how Scipio, the Roman general, captured the Carthaginian town of Nova Carthago in 209 BC.

3 'Scipio ordered, as the Romans usually do, that as the soldiers entered the city they should kill everyone they met and spare no-one. The purpose of this was to terrify everyone who heard of it. To show how fierce they were the Romans deliberately left chopped-up bodies on the streets.'

Polybius, second century BC

A Roman warship. The tall object (right) is a 'corvus', which can be lowered to form a gangplank by which the troops can move onto land or on board other ships.

1 There were three Punic Wars between Rome and Carthage. Explain in your own words what happened in each one.

2 Look at Source D. For each extract, work out what we can learn from Polybius about why the Romans won the Punic Wars. Put your findings on a table like this:

Extract	Reasons for Roman victory
1	
2	
3	

3 It is a pity that only one detailed account of the Punic Wars survives. How could this stop historians from making sense of the Punic Wars?

THE ROMAN ARMY AT WAR

> The Roman army won many battles and was able to conquer a large number of countries.
>
> *Why was the Roman army so successful?*

What causes can we find to explain why the Roman army did so well? Let's start by looking at the way in which the Roman army was organised. Think about why it is important for an army to be organised.

An organised army

In the early days, Rome was defended by part-time soldiers. By about 100 BC a stronger army was needed. The army was reorganised and it was now made up of full-time trained soldiers. The Romans had a very large army. All male Roman citizens between the ages of 17 and 46 could be called up as soldiers.

Soldiers were organised into large groups called legions. A legion was made up of about 5,000 men.

In the year AD 43, the year that the Romans conquered Britain, there were 27 legions in the whole Roman army. Four of these legions were used to invade Britain.

The officer commanding a legion was called the legate. Each legion was divided up into ten groups called cohorts. The cohorts were divided up into six centuries – units of 80 or 100 men. Each group shared a tent and a mule when they were on the march.

A modern idea of what a Roman legionary looked like. This is based on lots of different types of evidence.

17

Strong and healthy soldiers

The Romans had a clear idea about the importance of fitness and health.

● Do you think Vegetius' advice is good? Would a modern army handbook give the same sort of advice about choosing soldiers?

The fighting camp

When the Roman army was on the move, it regularly had to pitch a new camp. It was important to make the camp safe from enemy attacks.

A modern artist's impression of a Roman marching camp. The Roman army built temporary camps and permanent forts in important positions. The soldiers slept in leather tents.

Keeping order

All successful armies are run strictly so that soldiers do as they are told when it comes to war. The Roman army was stricter than those of its enemies. Soldiers who broke important rules were put to death as an example to other legionaries.

SOURCE C

A Greek writer described how soldiers were treated if they were guilty of a serious offence.

'An officer takes a baton and simply touches the man with it. This is a sign to all the other soldiers that they must stone or beat him to death.'

Polybius, second century BC

Machines of war

We have seen that the army was well organised, and discipline was strict. This obviously explains partly why the Roman army was successful. If we look at the way the Romans fought battles we might find some more clues to help explain why their army was so strong and powerful.

A soldier's sandals were as important as his armour, because the army needed to march quickly to the place of attack. The sandals were strong, and the nails on the sole were designed to carry weight over long distances.

SOURCE D

The Roman historian, Dio Cassius, describes a *testudo* formation.

'The legionaries face outwards with their shields and weapons ready. The others, densely packed in the square, raise their shields to cover their heads and interlock them. Nothing can be seen now except shields, and all the men are protected against missiles. This roof of shields is so amazingly strong that men can walk on it, indeed even horses and chariots can be driven over it.

The *testudo* is useful when they come to narrow passes. It is used in attacking forts for it enables the men to reach right up to the walls.'

Dio Cassius, about AD 200

SOURCE F

Vegetius, a Roman civil servant, wrote:

'The Roman legion is victorious because of its number of soldiers and the types of war machines it uses. It is equipped with ballistas – hurling machines – which can pierce body armour and shields.'

Vegetius, *De Re Militari*, fourth century AD

- Look at Sources D and E. How did the testudo formation help the Romans to attack fortified positions?

SOURCE E

Soldiers in a special formation called a 'testudo'. Testudo is the Latin word for tortoise. The Romans sometimes used this formation.

Inset: This scene is from Trajan's Column in Rome. The marble column was built in AD 113 by order of the Emperor Trajan in honour of lands he conquered in Romania.

SOURCE G

Julius Caesar describes a Roman attack.

'Our soldiers cleared a way by using slings, arrows and war engines. This helped our troops. The enemy were disturbed by the shape of the ships, by the beating of the oars and by the war engines. They were not used to the war engines. The enemy stood still and then took a few steps backward. The moment our men got a steady foothold on land, they made a mass charge and made the enemy run away.'

Julius Caesar, *The Gallic Wars*, 51–44 BC

SOURCE H

This is an account of an attack by the Roman army on the Etruscan city of Veii in 396 BC.

'Camillus split up the workers into six shifts, to work six hours each in turn. The operation was planned to continue without pause until the fortress was reached. The people of Veii had no idea that the Romans would burst through the tunnel.

The tunnel was now full of picked men. Suddenly they came bursting out, into the temple in the middle of the fortress. The men of Veii, looking outwards from the walls, were attacked from behind, bolts were wrenched off the gates and some of the Romans set fire to the houses. In a moment, men were being thrown off the walls and the gates were open. The rest of the Roman army poured in or climbed the undefended walls.'

Quoted in R. Nichols and K. McLeish, *Through Roman Eyes*, 1976

Communications

The army could move quickly because the Roman soldiers built first-class roads. When the Romans arrived in new lands, they found just winding tracks, which avoided natural obstacles like woods, hills and bogs. The Romans cut down woods, cut into hillsides and drained marshes to make their roads as straight as possible. This meant that troops and supplies could travel quickly from place to place. There is a map showing some of the Roman roads on page 35.

1 a In pairs, discuss the different reasons why the Roman army was so effective. Now fill in the following table. Number each item according to how important you think each factor (reason) is (from 1 to 6, most to least important).

How did these things help to make the Roman army strong?	
Organisation	
Health and fitness	
Camps and forts	
Discipline	
Weapons and tactics	
Communications	

b Compare your table with those of others in the class, and discuss the results.

c Can you think of any other reasons why the army was so successful?

2 'The Romans looked after their soldiers.' Do you agree? Give examples from as many sources as you can to explain your answer.

3 Which is the most useful source for historians trying to find out what it was like to be a Roman soldier?

4 Vegetius wrote that 'the survival of Rome depends on the kind of soldiers we choose'. What do you think he meant?

5 Using all the information that you have on the Roman army in this unit, explain why you agree or do not agree with this sentence:
'Roman tactics and weapons were very good. They were the main reason why the Romans won so many battles.'

V THE URGE TO CONQUER

The Romans built up an enormous empire from the Atlantic to the Indian Ocean.

Why did the Romans conquer so many countries? Why do people disagree about the motives of the Romans?

A sense of mission?

We have seen that the Romans built up a huge and mighty empire but we have not yet answered the question, 'Why did they do it?'

Historians use the word 'motive' to describe the reason why people do things. Let's read what some Roman writers had to say.

Source A is a small part of a very long poem called *The Aeneid*, by the Roman poet, Virgil. It tells the story of a legendary Trojan leader called Aeneas. Virgil was writing *The Aeneid* at the same time as Augustus was emperor, when the Roman Empire was very large (look at the map on pages 6–7). Augustus liked the poem very much.

SOURCE A

In this part of the story, Aeneas's father stands in the underworld and shows his son the spirits of men who will one day bring great things to the city of Rome.

'Remember, you are a Roman. It will be your job to rule over other countries, so that the world becomes peaceful, and everyone obeys the law.'

Virgil, *The Aeneid*, 29–19 BC

- What other reasons can you think of to explain why one person or group of people tries to take over another?

The spoils of war

Source B is from a history of Rome by the Roman writer, Livy. He was also writing at the time of the Emperor Augustus. In this extract he describes a Roman attack on a foreign city.

SOURCE B

'Paullus called for ten leading men from each city and told them to have the gold and silver brought out into the public squares. All the gold and silver was collected and at 10 o'clock the soldiers were given the signal to ransack the cities. Each foot soldier had a share worth a lot of money, while 150,000 people were led off into slavery.'

Livy's *History*, 29 BC–AD 17

SOURCE C

Ransacking a city for food and supplies. This is another scene from Trajan's Column built in AD 113.

Why did the Romans attack other peoples?

Romans wanted more wealth

SOURCE D

This is part of a speech which is supposed to have been made by a British chieftain who had come into contact with the Romans. It was written down by a Roman writer, Tacitus, who travelled widely in the Empire. (Tacitus may have made up the speech himself.)

'The Romans are the only men on earth who attack poor and rich with the same enthusiasm. Robbery, murder, rape are all disguised under the name "empire". They make a desert and call it "peace".'

Tacitus, *Agricola*, AD 98

1 Why did the Romans attack other peoples?
a In pairs, read Sources A, B and D, then see if you can find any more reasons or motives to add to the diagram above.
b Do any of the motives disagree with each other?
c Do any of the motives on the diagram seem difficult to believe? If so, why?

2 All the writers of the sources are Roman. Why does this make it difficult to find out about Roman motives?

3 Why do you think historians disagree about the reasons for the Roman conquest?

VI THE STRUGGLE FOR POWER

For many centuries Rome was a republic. It was ruled by two consuls and the rich men of the Senate. There was no one single person in charge. In 46 BC, the republic came to an end when the famous general, Julius Caesar, seized power. He started to rule like a dictator.

Why did the republic fall apart?

In 46 BC Julius Caesar became the most powerful person in Rome. To understand why the republic fell apart and Julius Caesar came to power, we need to look at what happened in his lifetime. We also need to look back at changes that happened much earlier.

For a long time the power of the Senate was threatened by two things: the power of the army, and the hatred of the poor.

The army and the power of the generals

In the early years the Romans had a part-time army. Most of the soldiers were farmers and when the fighting was over they returned to their farms. As the area under Roman control grew, it became difficult to keep this system going.

Around the year 100 BC a general called Marius reorganised the army and made it a full-time, professional force. Full-time soldiers saw their jobs in a different light. If they had a general who was good to them, they would be very loyal to him. They were loyal even to the point of fighting against the government of Rome when their general ordered them. This gave massive power to the generals. Generals like Marius became very proud. If he disagreed with the senators in Rome, Marius was ready to march his soldiers to the city to force the politicians to change their mind.

Marius died in 86 BC. After his death a number of other generals also argued with the government of Rome. Civil war broke out in 83–82 BC. The winner of this war was a soldier called Sulla. He treated his rivals in a ruthless and brutal way.

SOURCE A

This is a description of how Sulla dealt with his enemies at the end of the war in 82 BC.

'Some threw their weapons away and were taken prisoner. They were locked up in the Villa Publica on the Campus Martius. There were 3,000 or 4,000 of them. After three days Sulla sent his soldiers in and slaughtered them all.'

Strabo, 7 BC

● What sort of a man was the general Sulla?

After the death of Sulla in 78 BC, another strong general began to dominate Rome. He was Pompey. For many years Pompey and the young Julius Caesar were allies. But later they quarrelled, and in 49 BC Caesar and his soldiers began to fight Pompey and his men. By 46 BC this new civil war was over and Pompey had been murdered. Caesar was now all-powerful in Rome. Two years later he became 'dictator for life'.

The poor become more angry

The century before Caesar came to power was a time of great hatred between rich and poor Romans. This hatred was another reason why the old system of the republic fell apart. Small farms found it difficult to make much money, and farming families often sold up and moved to Rome. There were not many jobs in Rome so the new people from the countryside were very poor.

At the same time a few Romans became massively rich. The well-off Romans built up huge new farms, or estates, that were worked by large numbers of slaves.

The rich Romans were divided among themselves. Some wanted to help the poor, others did not. In 133 BC a man called Gracchus said that the poor should be given land taken from the rich. A group of leading rich senators murdered him. Ten years later they killed his brother for wanting to help the poor.

The murder of the Gracchus brothers made poor Romans feel even more bitter. They were happy to support any leader who would take power from rich men in the Senate, and promise them a better way of life. One such man was Julius Caesar.

THE REPUBLIC
Rome was ruled by the Senate, a group of rich men. They took turns at the most important jobs.

THE ARMY

Being a soldier meant working full-time. The Soldiers supported their general, not the Senate. Generals became very powerful.

THE POOR
There was a great increase in the number of poor Romans. They hated the rich men in the Senate.

The way was open for a powerful general - who would help the poor - to take over from the Senate.

Crisis for the republic.

---

1 a How did the Roman army change around the year 100 BC?
b How did these changes make generals very powerful?

2 Explain in your own words how the rich got richer while the poor got poorer in the years before Caesar's take-over.

3 What clues have you been able to find in this unit to explain why the Roman republic started to fall apart in these years?

JULIUS CAESAR,
MASTER OF ROME

In 46 BC, Julius Caesar became ruler of the Roman world. He was helped by the long-standing problems of the army and the poor. But these factors alone are not enough to explain his success. We must also look at the sort of person he was.

What was Julius Caesar like? How did this help him to take power?

Victory in Gaul

Julius Caesar was born about 100 BC. Although he came from a wealthy background, he was always keen to win the support of the poor. After a series of important jobs, he was given command of the Roman armies in Gaul (modern France) in 58 BC. He was a very successful general and soon conquered the whole of Gaul. In 55 BC he also raided Britain.

Look at the rest of this unit to find out more about Caesar's personality.

SOURCE A

Suetonius was secretary to the Emperor Hadrian. He carefully used government records to help him write his book about the first Roman emperors.

'Caesar chose Gaul because it was the most likely place to give him wealth and triumphs [the greatest honour a general could get was to lead his troops "in triumph" back into the centre of Rome].

He picked quarrels — however unfair and dangerous — and marched against enemy tribes. The more battles he won, the more public holidays the people of Rome got. Caesar made the people of Gaul pay 400,000 gold pieces in taxes every year. He also raided Britain, a previously unknown country, and made the people there pay a lot of taxes.

He began building a new forum in Rome with all this money. Then he put on a gladiator show. He doubled the wages of the army.

Every infantryman was given a farm. Food was given out to the people. Stage plays, chariot races and mock naval battles were held after his victories.

In Gaul he stole statues from temples. He even stole 3,000 lb of gold from Rome.

He was a skilful swordsman and horseman. He always led his army, more often on foot than in the saddle. He did not allow his army to be ambushed. He checked the position of his enemies carefully. If a soldier turned back in battle, Caesar would catch him by the throat and force him to face the enemy again.

If his troops looked likely to panic, he might make a speech to them. Deserters were heavily punished. When they won a battle he allowed his troops to enjoy themselves. When a group of his soldiers were massacred, he promised that he would not cut his hair or shave his beard until he had got revenge.'

Suetonius, AD 130

Public speaking – oratory – was a very important subject at Roman schools. Boys watched their fathers make speeches.

SOURCE B

Cicero was a Roman senator, orator and writer. He heard some of Caesar's greatest speeches.

'Do you know any man who can speak better than Caesar – even if he had spent all his time learning oratory? Or anyone who makes so many clever remarks? Or whose words are so cleverly chosen?'

Letter from Cicero (who lived from 106 to 43 BC) to his friend Cornelius Nepos

SOURCE C

The historian Asinius Pollio was with Caesar's army at the Rubicon and wrote down what happened.

'When he came to the Rubicon he began to think about what a huge and terrible thing he was about to do. For a long time he talked with the friends who were with him. Finally he stopped thinking and made a leap into the future, saying, as men often do when they're going to do something desperate, "Let's throw the dice." Then he crossed the river.'

Pollio (he lived from 76 BC to AD 5)

By crossing the river with his army, Caesar led his soldiers to war with Rome. In the civil war that followed, Caesar emerged as winner – the master of Rome.

● Caesar's action has given us the expression 'crossing the Rubicon'. Can you find out what it means today?

● Why do you think it was so important for Caesar to be a good speaker?

Crossing the Rubicon

Julius Caesar was due to end his time as Governor of Gaul in the year 49 BC. His enemy, Pompey, was worried that Caesar would march his army into Rome and take power for himself. Caesar's enemies in the Senate in Rome made it clear that if Caesar brought his soldiers into Italy, he would be breaking the law, and they would try to kill him.

Caesar had to decide whether to risk crossing the River Rubicon, which marked the border of Italy, or to stay in Gaul.

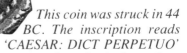

This coin was struck in 44 BC. The inscription reads 'CAESAR: DICT PERPETUO' (Caesar, Dictator for Life). It shows Caesar wearing the laurel wreath, a symbol of victory and peace. Roman emperors wore the laurel wreath instead of a gold crown, because they did not want to be thought of as 'king'.

The Ides of March

Caesar did not live long to enjoy his supreme control of Rome. He was hated by those rich people who wanted Rome to be run in the old way, with the Senate in charge. There were many rumours of plots to kill him. One fortune-teller told Caesar that he should 'beware the Ides of March'. This was the Roman name for the 15th of March. Caesar ignored the warning. On 15 March 44 BC he was knifed to death by a group of leading Romans, led by a former friend called Marcus Brutus. Caesar died with twenty-three dagger wounds in his body.

Brutus and the other killers wanted to get rid of Caesar because he was acting like a dictator.

The sheer drama of Caesar's murder has gripped people's imagination ever since. In the late sixteenth century, William Shakespeare wrote the play 'Julius Caesar', which is often performed today. This painting of the assassination is by Vincenzo Camuccini (1773–1844).

The murder was not very successful, though. Caesar's friends and relations soon wanted revenge. Within three years most of the killers had been put to death. Eventually Caesar's adopted son, Augustus, took over and became the first emperor.

---

1 Write down two facts and two opinions about Julius Caesar from the sources in this unit.

2 Why do you think modern historians still disagree about what sort of man Julius Caesar was?

3 Explain in detail:
a what you think about Caesar's personality
b how you think his personality helped him to the top in Roman politics.

VIII AUGUSTUS:
THE FIRST EMPEROR

Augustus was the first Emperor of Rome. He came to power a number of years after Julius Caesar's sudden death in 44 BC. He ruled the empire until he died at the age of 76. Augustus's rule was remembered as a successful period in Roman history. Whilst Caesar had seized power, but could not hold on to it, Augustus managed to hold on to power for over forty years.

What made Augustus such a successful leader?

Who was Augustus?

Before we look at evidence about Augustus, think about what sort of person makes a good leader. What do you think the most important qualities are?

● Make a list of some famous leaders today. What words do you think describe a successful leader?

At the time of Caesar's death, Augustus was only 18 years old and studying in Greece. He was the great-nephew and adopted son of Caesar.

When Julius Caesar was killed, there were a number of men in a good position to take over from him. One of these was Caesar's friend, Mark Antony. Another was Augustus.

How did Augustus come to power?

When Augustus heard the news that Julius Caesar had been stabbed to death, he wanted to get his own back. He returned to Rome and joined forces with Mark Antony in 42 BC to defeat the murderers, Brutus and Cassius. Then Augustus and Mark Antony divided up the empire. Augustus took the west and Antony ruled the east.

Antony soon fell in love with Cleopatra, the Queen of Egypt. He led a life of luxury at her court. Augustus grew angry with him for neglecting his duties to the empire. In 31 BC Augustus declared war, and there was a great sea battle at Actium (off modern Greece). Antony killed himself after he lost the battle.

Cleopatra killed herself by allowing a snake to bite her. The rivals of Augustus were now out of the way. Augustus was the sole ruler of the Roman Empire.

Once Augustus had got rid of his enemies he still had to hold on to his power. What problems did he face? Which groups of people did he need to keep happy so that they would support him?

'How do I stay in power?' This diagram shows some of the things Augustus had to do to stay in charge of the Roman Empire. Add as many of your own ideas as you can.

29

Augustus in power

Augustus was careful not to call himself King. He knew that the Roman people did not like the idea of a king: it reminded them of the old stories of the early kings of Rome.

Augustus tried to show that he respected the Senate. He allowed the senators to carry on discussing laws as they had always done. He or one of his friends was usually chosen to be consul. So he was clever enough to keep the Senate happy.

In return, the Senate allowed him really to run the government. When some people began to worship him as a god, Augustus did not complain.

Sometimes Augustus was nicknamed 'Imperator', which means commander. This is the origin of the title Emperor. Augustus stayed in charge of the army and rewarded soldiers for being loyal.

During the reign of Augustus there were fewer wars. The Roman Empire was largely at peace. Civil servants were trained to run the provinces in the empire. Money from taxes was spent on strong and glorious buildings throughout the Roman lands. Many new roads were built to link the provinces with each other and with Rome.

SOURCE A

When Augustus died in AD 14, he left a large inscription in Rome telling the story of the things he did when he was Emperor.

'I repaired the aqueducts and eighty-two temples. I gave three gladiator shows at which 10,000 fought. I brought peace to Gaul, Spain, Germany and many other places. I added Egypt to the Empire. The people gave me the title of Father of the Country.'

From *Works of the Divine Augustus,* written by Augustus before his death in AD 14

SOURCE B

The Roman historian Tacitus loved freedom, so it was important for him to explain why people in the Roman Empire accepted having so little freedom under the rule of Augustus.

'After the battle of Actium all power had to be put in the hands of one man for the sake of peace. First Augustus won over the army with gifts. Then he won over the poor people with cheap corn and the delights of peace. Rich men became even richer as they accepted their slavery.'

From *Annals* by Tacitus (who lived from AD 55 to 117)

SOURCE C

The Roman historian Suetonius describes how the emperor treated his enemies, including Brutus, killer of Julius Caesar.

'He showed no mercy to his beaten enemies. He sent Brutus' head to Rome to be thrown at the feet of Caesar's statue ... After he had captured the city of Perusia, Augustus told all those prisoners who begged for mercy: "You must die." '

Suetonius, *Augustus,* AD 130

1 Using the information and sources in this unit, explain why Augustus was thought to be a successful leader. The more examples you give, the better.

Source
What type of source is it?
Who produced it?
When was it produced?
What does it tell us about Augustus?
How is Augustus shown?
Why might Augustus want to be shown like this?

SOURCE D

This is a poem written for Augustus by the Roman poet Horace. It describes Augustus as

'all conquering in war, and
    yet not unfair
To those he conquers . . .
Now Trust, Peace and Self
    Respect and Decency have
    returned
At last to Rome . . .'

Carmen Saeculare by Horace (he lived from 65 to 8 BC)

● Does the fact that Horace was paid by Augustus to write the poem in Source E affect your view of this source?

2 Complete this table using the sources in the unit. Explain which sources are the most useful for finding out about Augustus.

3 Do you think any of the sources are unreliable? Explain your answer.

A	B	C	D	E

SOURCE E

A marble statue of Augustus, about AD 14, the year he died. His wife ordered the statue to be made and it was put in the garden of her villa. Augustus is shown as a Roman general speaking to his soldiers. The breastplate shows Apollo the sun god.

31

THE ROMAN EMPERORS

AUGUSTUS I   31 BC–AD 14

HE DEFEATED MARK ANTONY AT THE BATTLE OF ACTIUM IN 31 BC. AND BECAME THE FIRST EMPEROR OF ROME. HIS LONG REIGN WAS THE BEGINNING OF A PERIOD OF PEACE WHICH LASTED FOR ABOUT 200 YEARS.

HADRIAN   AD 117–138

AS EMPEROR. HE TRAVELLED WIDELY AROUND THE EMPIRE. HE TRIED TO SECURE ITS LONG BORDERS WITH WALLS AND FORTIFICATIONS AGAINST ENEMY ATTACKS. HE BUILT HADRIAN'S WALL IN BRITAIN TO PROTECT IT FROM NORTH BRITISH TRIBES.

44 BC **31 BC**   **AD14**   **37-41**   **117** /**138**   **180** **192**
Death of Caesar

CALIGULA   AD 37–41

HE WAS THE SON OF GERMANICUS. HE WAS NOTED FOR HIS EXTREME CRUELTY AND MADNESS. HE EVEN MADE HIS HORSE A CONSUL. AND BUILT A SPECIAL PALACE FOR IT. HE WAS ASSASSINATED IN AD 41.

COMMODUS   AD 180–192

HE WAS LAZY. INCOMPETENT. AND KNOWN FOR HIS VICIOUS TYRANNY. HE LIKED TO ENJOY HIMSELF. HE WAS STRANGLED BY HIS SOLDIERS. WHO ALSO KILLED THE NEXT EMPEROR. AND THEN SOLD THE TITLE TO THE HIGHEST BIDDER.

AT A GLANCE

50 EMPERORS   AD 235-284

DURING THIS PERIOD THERE WERE MORE THAN 50 EMPERORS. ONE WAS CAPTURED BY THE PERSIANS. ONE DIED OF PLAGUE, AND MANY MET A VIOLENT END. THE MAIN REASON FOR SO MANY EMPERORS WAS THAT THE ARMY SUPPORTED THOSE WHO PAID THEM WELL.

CONSTANTINE THE GREAT   AD 306-337

CONSTANTINE CAME FROM THE REGION OF THE EMPIRE THAT IS NOW CALLED YUGOSLAVIA. HE BECAME EMPEROR OF A REUNITED EMPIRE. IN AD 313 HE MADE CHRISTIANITY THE OFFICIAL RELIGION OF THE ROMAN EMPIRE. HE WAS THE FIRST CHRISTIAN ROMAN EMPEROR.

235   284   305-306   337   379   395

DIOCLETIAN   AD 284-305

HE MADE GREAT EFFORTS TO REORGANISE THE ROMAN EMPIRE. HE DIVIDED IT INTO FOUR PARTS TO MAKE IT EASIER TO RUN. HE PERSECUTED MANY CHRISTIANS IN AD 303. THIS WAS THE LAST TIME THAT THEY WERE TREATED SEVERELY IN THE EMPIRE.

THEODOSIUS   AD 379-395

FROM AD 395 THE ROMAN EMPIRE WAS PERMANENTLY DIVIDED INTO TWO HALVES, EAST AND WEST. HE WAS EMPEROR OF THE EASTERN HALF OF THE EMPIRE.

ON THE ROAD

The Roman Empire was covered by a vast network of roads. They were so well made that many modern roads still follow the very straight route of an original Roman route.

Why were roads so important to the Romans?

Soldiers and transport

All the main Roman roads were at first built by the army. It was only by moving soldiers and equipment quickly that the huge empire could be kept under control.

SOURCE A

The writings of Julius Caesar make it clear how vital good communications were for the Roman army.

'When I heard that the Helvetii [a tribe near Lake Geneva] planned to enter Roman territory, I hurriedly left Rome for Gaul, and, travelling with all possible speed, reached the area around Geneva. There was only one legion in Gaul so I gave orders for the bridge at Geneva to be destroyed and defences to be built. Then I travelled as fast as I could back to Italy where I obtained five more legions and marched them back to Gaul across the Alps. Despite attacks from various tribes we completed this journey in seven days.'

Julius Caesar, *The Gallic Wars*, describing the years 58–52 BC

Governing the Empire

When the army had won firm control over an area, the roads became important for linking the local government in the provinces to the central government in Rome. The roads were also important for the official postal system. On each main road there were stables every ten to fifteen kilometres where messengers could change horses, and there were official guest-houses every thirty to forty kilometres. In an age long before cars and trains, people on government business could still travel very fast by horse or carriage. Emperor Tiberius, for example, once covered 300 kilometres in one day.

Roads and the traders

Soon after they were built, traders started to make use of the roads. As you can see from the map, different parts of the empire specialised in making particular goods. These were transported either by road or by sea.

- 'All roads lead to Rome.' Does the map opposite help to make sense of this expression, which we still use today?

THE ROMAN EMPIRE

KILOMETRES 0 500

London
Lyon
Aquilea
Marseille
Tarragon
Byzantium
(Constantinople)
ROME
Brindisi
Mediterranean Sea
Cadiz
Tangier
Corinth
Antioch
Carthage
Alexandria
Tyre

wine
corn
olive oil
cloth/wool
purple dye

metals
marble
ivory
wild beasts

——— main roads
- - - main sea routes
       Roman Empire

jewels, spices + perfumes from the East ↑

SOURCE B

Jo-Ann Shelton is a modern historian who has investigated the Roman way of life.

'Any large town has to deal with the problems of bringing in supplies and taking out goods for sale. Rome's economy, government and army depended on a system of roads throughout the empire. These well-built roads allowed Romans to get to any part of the empire quickly and transport supplies, businessmen, messengers, civil servants or soldiers cheaply and safely.'

Jo-Ann Shelton, *As the Romans Did*, 1988

SOURCE C

A Greek called Aelius Aristides describes what happened when trading ships arrived in Rome from other parts of the empire.

'So many trading ships arrive in Rome with cargoes from everywhere, at all times of the year, and after each harvest, that the city seems like the world's warehouse. The arrival and departure never stops – it's amazing that the sea, not to mention the harbour, is big enough for these trading ships.'

Aelius Aristides, second century AD

A journey by road

Journeys by road were not always easy. The grandest of all Roman roads was the Appian Way. It ran 377 kilometres from Rome to the port of Brindisi. The Roman poet Horace described a journey the length of the Appian Way.

'With my friends I set out from Rome on the road for Brindisi. On the second day we reached the town of Forum Appii. The town was packed with boatmen for the river crossing, and money-grabbing inn-keepers. The water they gave us was bad and I was sick.

Soon it was night and the boatmen and their slaves started shouting and bawling. We had to wait an hour for them to collect the fares and harness our mule. On the way across the river our boatman, who was drunk, fell asleep until a passenger started to beat him over the head and back-side with a willow branch. After finally reaching the other side we crawled slowly three miles up to the city of Anxur, set high on its glittering rocks.

We travelled on to Beneventum. There the inn-keeper fussed about so much that he nearly burnt the house down while he was cooking some skinny thrushes on the fire. There were flames everywhere, leaping up to lick at the roof. Hungry guests and terrified slaves had to snatch up their dinners and try to put out the flames.

Next we came to the good old hills of Apulia. Then we went by carriage and quickly covered twenty-four miles to the next town. There you actually had to pay for water. From there we had a long and weary journey through pouring rain. Next day the weather was better but the road was worse. Finally we reached Brindisi.'

Horace (he lived from 65 to 8 BC)

A modern artist's impression of the Appian Way, near Rome. The road still exists today.

1 a Make a list of problems that people face travelling on modern roads.
b Look at Sources A and D. What problems did these travellers on Roman roads face?
c Which do you think the more dangerous: travelling by road today, or in Roman times?

2 a Using evidence from this unit, make a list of the different reasons for using Roman roads.
b Which of these reasons was the most important?

3 The writers of Sources A and D were very rich and powerful. Do you think poor people used the roads in the same way?

THE ROMAN BUILDERS

The Romans were great builders. They covered their empire with new towns, bridges and roads. Many of the buildings were so well made that they have survived for 2,000 years.

How did the Roman builders work?

SOURCE A

The Colosseum, a huge amphitheatre in Rome. It was built in the first century AD. It could hold about 45,000 spectators who came to watch gladiators and wild beasts fighting. The building was a great achievement. As well as being three tiers high, there were deep cells and cellars below.

SOURCE C

The Pont du Gard, built in France in the first century AD. This great aqueduct brought water to Nîmes from 40 kilometres away. Some people say that it is a work of art as well as a feat of engineering. The section here is about 275 metres long. It has a water channel running on the top level, about 55 metres above the river below.

Slaves, legionaries and engineers

Some important building work was done by the army. All legions were expected to help at times with building, and some legions had specialist building craftsmen. Other projects were undertaken by civilians (people who were not in the army). The workforce was often a mixture of slaves, who did the dirtiest, heaviest work, and free labourers. They were organised by engineers who usually designed the plans and supervised the building.

A revolution in stone

Before the Romans, stone buildings were rare in Europe. In the Roman Empire, stone was used very widely. Even the smallest towns had stone-built temples, bath-houses, theatres and an amphitheatre. The Roman builders were skilled at constructing 'dry' walls without cement, but when they wanted to they could make a strong mortar. They also knew how to make bricks and concrete.

The engineers were clearly very skilful and precise. However, they were not very good at developing new machinery. They seemed happy with the simple machines they had. One reason for this was that they had lots of workers, and so did not need to develop much technology.

SOURCE B

The Roman writer Pliny the Younger was governor of Bithynia in modern Turkey. He wrote to the Emperor Trajan, asking for permission to build a canal.

'Connecting the lake with the sea will be a big job but there is no shortage of labour in this area. A good supply of men is available in the countryside and still more in the town. It seems certain that everyone will take part in something that helps everybody.'

Letters of Pliny the Younger, second century AD

Source D

We can get an idea of the energy of the Roman builders from some of the books written in praise of the emperors.

'On behalf of the Emperor Probus the army built bridges, temples and public buildings. They dredged the mouths of the rivers, drained many marshes and created fields and farms in their place.'

Historia Augusta, third century AD

Source E

Although there were many great achievements, things could go wrong.

'The citizens of Nicomedia [in modern Turkey] have spent huge sums of money trying to build an aqueduct. Building started twice, but twice it had to be demolished and they are still without water.'

Letters of Pliny, second century AD

---

1 In what ways were Roman buildings different from earlier buildings in Europe?

2 'Roman builders did not use complicated machinery. This means they were not very clever.' Would you agree with this statement?

3 What differences and similarities can you find between modern buildings and Roman buildings?

XI FAMILY LIFE

> Family life was very important to the Romans. Men were the most powerful people in the family.
>
> **What was life like for men, women and children in a Roman family?**

A wealthy family. This diagram is based on the work of a modern historian.

Father

☆ Had a strong control over his wife and family.
☆ Preferred to have sons to daughters.
☆ Sometimes left newborn babies, particularly girls, to die.

Mother

☆ Often died in childbirth at a young age.
☆ Could be married off in her early teens and be a grandmother by the age of 30.
☆ Ran the family and household when the father was away.
☆ Was not supposed to get involved in politics.
☆ Enjoyed some freedom and respect.

Children

☆ Were quite likely to die of disease before becoming teenagers.
☆ Might be given away, or adopted by another family.
☆ Boys with rich parents were well educated.
☆ Girls could be married off at the age of 13.

Slaves

☆ Were not protected by the law. The master could work them as hard as he wanted.
☆ Could be tortured or even killed by their master.
☆ Could be set free for good service.
☆ A wealthy family owned dozens of slaves. Even a poor Roman family usually owned one.

The power of the father

In a Roman family the father was usually looked upon as the most important person. He owned everything that the family had. His children could not get married without his permission. His word was obeyed, even by his grown-up sons and daughters.

Women, even when they were married, were still thought to be part of their father's family. This meant that in Roman law, a husband could be over-ruled by his wife's father. Wives were allowed to keep their own money and could divorce their husbands if they wanted to.

Family life for slaves was very different. A slave family could be split up, because a master could sell off members of the family to others. Even if slaves worked for a family all their lives, they were rarely considered part of the family they worked for.

Your job is to look at the evidence of the sources in this unit (pages 41–43). See if it supports the views of the modern historian shown in the diagram opposite.

1 a Which sources support the idea that babies might be left to die?
b Which sources support the idea that people died young in the Roman period?
c Which sources support the idea that girls married very young during the Roman period?

2 a Only one written source is by a woman. Why do you think that is?
b What problems does this cause historians?

3 Make up three questions about any aspect of Roman family life that can be answered by these sources. Do not use the ones above. Then get a friend to answer them in writing.

4 According to the sources, are the statements in the diagram about Roman family life generally 'true' or 'false'? Explain your answer in detail.

SOURCE B

'Even the rich and the very wealthy leave children to die so that the remaining children should have more money.'

From a book called *Reliquiae*, by Musonius Rufus, who lived in either the first or second century AD

SOURCE C

Juvenal was a Roman writer famous for his opinion about all aspects of life.

'I hate a woman who reads.'

From *Satires* by Juvenal, written in the first century AD

Much information about family life comes from inscriptions on tombstones.

SOURCE D

'SACRED TO THE DEPARTED SPIRIT OF JULIA SATURNINA, 45 YEARS OLD, A GOOD WIFE, EXCELLENT DOCTOR AND MOST HONEST WOMAN. CASSIUS HER HUSBAND MADE THIS MONUMENT.'

Tombstone at Emerista, Spain

SOURCE F

'I WAS CALLED, WHILE ALIVE, AURELIA . . . MY HUSBAND, WHOM, ALAS, I NOW HAVE LEFT, WAS A FELLOW FREE-MAN. HE WAS TRULY LIKE A FATHER TO ME. WHEN I WAS SEVEN YEARS OLD HE EMBRACED ME. NOW I AM FORTY AND IN THE POWER OF DEATH. THROUGH MY CONSTANT CARE, MY HUSBAND FLOURISHED.'

Tombstone in Rome, first century BC

SOURCE E

'TO THE SPIRITS OF THE DEPARTED, ANTIATILIANUS AGED 10, PROTUS AGED 12, POMPEIUS OPTATUS, THEIR MASTER, HAD THIS MADE.'

Tombstone at Chester, England

SOURCE G

'TO THE SPIRITS OF THE DEPARTED AND OF YLAS, HIS DEAREST FOSTER-CHILD AGED 13, CLAUDIUS SEVERUS, MILITARY TRIBUNE, SET THIS UP.'

Tombstone at Old Penrith, England

42

Source H

A scene from a carved relief, showing a Roman lady surrounded by her maids.

Source I

Slaves could not be sure of having a normal family life under the Romans. The Roman Emperor Theodosius II made the following law.

'Who can put up with children being separated from their parents, sisters from brothers, wives from husbands? Therefore anyone who has separated slaves and dragged them off to a different owner must recover these slaves and place them with one single owner.'

From the *Law Code of Theodosius*, AD 438

Source J

A letter from a man called Hilarion to his wife.

'To Alis many greetings. If you give birth – the best of everything to you ! – and if it is a boy, look after it , but if it is a girl, let it die.'

Found at Oxyrhynchus, Egypt, I BC

Source K

This letter is from a mother to her grown-up son.

'. . . if you know that you are not well, write to me, and I will come to you. Don't forget to write about your health, for you know how worried mothers get about their children. Your children send love and greetings.'

A papyrus letter written in the third century AD

Source L

In 63 BC a number of wealthy Romans planned to take over the government. They were found out and arrested. One of the supporters of the group was a woman.

'Sempronia had often in the past acted as bravely as a man. She studied Greek and Latin literature. She could play the lyre and dance . . . She was so filled with burning lust that she more often made advances to men than they did to her . . . She could write poetry, be amusing. In fact, she was a woman of great wit and charm.'

From *The Conspiracy of Cataline* by Sallust (who lived from 86 to 34 BC)

XII SLAVERY

The Roman world depended on the use of slaves. They could be seen in every part of the empire, doing all sorts of jobs from doctor to gladiator fighter.

How well did the Romans treat their slaves?

Where did the slaves come from?

Slavery was known all over the Mediterranean in Roman times. Until the third century BC there were not many slaves in Rome. This changed when the Romans started conquering new lands. Many slaves were people who were captured during these wars, when their towns or countries were taken over by the Romans. For example, when the Romans won a great victory at Epirus in 167 BC, 150,000 slaves were taken and brought to Rome. They reached Rome's harbour at Ostia and were then sold in large slave markets. Bidding could be fierce.

People became slaves for other reasons too. Some slaves were criminals. Others were children who had been left to die by their families. Another group had been sold by parents who could not afford to feed them. Once the system of slavery had begun, large numbers of people were born into slavery.

How were the slaves treated?

Look at the following sources about how the Romans treated their slaves.

SOURCE A

This is a description of slaves who worked at a flour mill.

'These poor undersized slaves. Their skin was black and blue with bruises, their backs covered with cuts from the whip. They were covered with rags, not clothes, and it was hardly enough to make them decent. They had been branded on the forehead and half their hair was shaved off. On their legs they wore iron chains.'

Apuleius, about AD 157

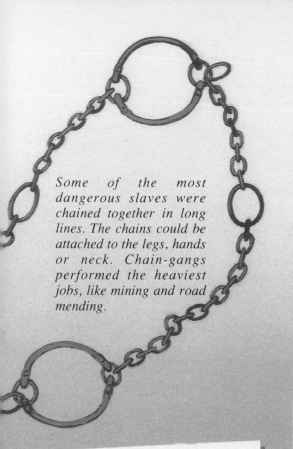

Some of the most dangerous slaves were chained together in long lines. The chains could be attached to the legs, hands or neck. Chain-gangs performed the heaviest jobs, like mining and road mending.

SOURCE B

This small figure, which is actually about 10 cm high, was found at Aldeburgh in Suffolk. It is a Roman oil pot made of bronze, and shows a sleepy young slave boy waiting for his master.

● Who do you think might have made this pot? Why?

SOURCE C

Some of the rich Romans who owned farms wrote about the way they farmed. Slaves are mentioned in some of these books. This piece was written by Cato, who lived between 234 and 149 BC. He was a writer, historian and orator as well as a farm owner. Here he describes the amount of clothes given to his slaves.

'Clothes: A tunic 1¼ metres long, and a cloak, every two years. Whenever you issue a new tunic or cloak, take back the old one for patching. You should see that each slave gets a good pair of clogs every second year.'

Cato, *On Farming*, 140 BC

SOURCE D

This is the view of some modern historians.

'If a slave fell sick or grew old, for example, he was no more use to his owner than a broken cooking-pot. "Business-like" masters sent some to the arena to feed the lions, or left them to die; others were often executed on the spot.'

R. Nichols and K. McLeish, *Through Roman Eyes*, 1976

SOURCE E

Most rich Roman writers also owned slaves. Varro was a Roman writer who lived from 116 to 27 BC. He wrote down some advice on farming

'There are three types of farm equipment. There is the kind that speaks (i.e. slave), the kind that cannot speak (i.e. cattle), and the voiceless (i.e. farm implements).'

Varro, *On Agriculture*, first century BC

Source F

Mosaic of gladiators, who were trained to fight in public shows with animals and other gladiators.

Source G

The Roman writer Pliny wrote many letters to his friends about all sorts of things. This letter includes his thoughts about how to treat slaves.

'I am always very upset when my slaves fall ill and die, especially the younger ones – but I am able to set them free before they die. I also allow slaves to make a will.'

Pliny the Younger, *Letters*, AD 97–109

Source H

The Roman writer Varro described the best way to treat slaves.

'You should not let your workers' spirits get too low – or too high. Don't let the foremen use whips, if they can get the same results with encouragement. Don't buy too many slaves from the same country – they argue with each other. You will find your slaves work better if you treat them well, or give them extra food or clothing, days off or permission to graze their cattle on your land.'

Varro, *On Agriculture*, first century BC

● Does Varro think it is *wrong* to use whips on slaves?

Source I

Slaves could be freed. The Emperor Claudius gave freed slaves jobs in the government. The Roman historian Suetonius described how Claudius treated freed slaves.

'Claudius put the freedman Felix in charge of the army and chose him to be governor of Judaea. When Harpocras was free he put on gladiator shows. But the Emperor's greatest favourites were his personal assistant, Narcissus, and his court treasurer, Pallas. These men made huge fortunes in money.'

Suetonius, *Lives of the Caesars*, AD 130

The slaves fight back

Look back at the diagram on page 13. It shows the main groups or classes of people who lived in Rome when Augustus was emperor. Notice where the slaves are on the diagram. Can you see why it has been drawn as a pyramid?

● Why do you think many Roman citizens were so worried about the danger of slave riots?

Archaeologists have found chains like the one on pages 44–45. Do you think this gives us any clues to help explain why there were slave revolts?

Spartacus and the slave revolt

In 73 BC a group of slaves at a gladiator school near Naples protested about their living conditions and ran away. They were led by a slave called Spartacus. They were joined by other slaves and formed themselves into a huge slave army. They wandered around the countryside and terrorised many citizens. It took two years and a powerful Roman army to crush the revolt. At the end of the struggle, 6,000 slaves who had been recaptured were crucified on crosses along the Appian Way, the main road from Rome to Capua.

● Read the story of Spartacus above. Why do you think the Roman government used such an awful punishment? Does this prove the Romans were cruel to their slaves?

---

1 What evidence can you find in the sources to show that
a some slaves were badly treated,
b some slaves were well treated?

2 How can you explain the fact that the sources say different things about how slaves were treated?

3 Source D comes from a modern history book. Is it more or less useful than the other sources, which come from Roman times?

4 Many people today think that 'the Romans treated their slaves like animals'. Do you agree?

ROMAN CITIES:

FINE OR FOUL?

The Romans have a reputation for being very well organised, and caring a lot about the health of their people. How true is this reputation?

How pleasant and healthy was life in a Roman city?

The large illustration below is an artist's idea of what the centre of Rome looked like in AD 330. As the city grew, many of the brick buildings were replaced by stone. Public toilets were built in the streets, at the baths and at the military forts. By AD 315 it is thought that Rome had 144 public toilets flushed by water. Rich people had running water and toilets put into their homes.

The Romans tried to provide public health for all their people. They had Water Inspectors, whose job was to make sure that the city had good supplies of clean water and efficient drains.

Source B shows some of the problems of sharing out the water.

Reconstruction of the centre of Rome, about AD 330.

SOURCE A

Part of the latrines at a Roman camp near Hadrian's Wall in England. The stone tubs in the centre were probably used for washing, and the water ran away along the drainage channels.

SOURCE B

Julius Frontinus was the Water Inspector for Rome. He describes how the water was shared out.

'The inspector must make sure that no one draws more water from the public system than he has permission for from the emperor. He must be on his guard all the time against cheats.

Water for the emperor 17.1%
For private people's houses and for industry 38.6%
Public supplies:
   19 army barracks 2.9%
   95 official buildings 24.1%
   39 baths and theatres 3.9%
'Stolen' water 13.4%
Total 100%'

Frontinus, *The Water Supply of Rome*, AD 97

SOURCE C

The writer Pliny the Elder lived for part of his life in Rome.

'Old men still admire the city sewers, the greatest achievement of all. They were built 700 years ago and they are still undamaged. Hills were tunnelled and Rome became like a hanging city. There are seven rivers made to flow in seven tunnels under the city. These finally run into one great sewer. These rivers rush through like mountain streams and, swollen by rain water, they sweep away all the sewage.'

Pliny the Elder, about AD 79

SOURCE D

Strabo was a Greek geographer who spent part of his life in Rome.

'Water is brought to the city in such quantities through the aqueducts that it is like a river flowing through the city.'

Strabo, *Geography*, first century BC

SOURCE E

Seneca was a Roman writer.

'I live over the public baths — you know what that means. Ugh! It's sickening. First there are the "strongmen" doing their exercises and swinging heavy lead weights about with grunts and groans. Next there are the lazy ones having a cheap massage — I can hear someone being slapped on the shoulders. Then there is the noise of a brawler or a thief being arrested, and the man who always likes the sound of his own voice in the bath. And what about the ones who leap into the pool making a huge splash as they hit the water!'

Seneca, around AD 63

Reconstruction of a street in ancient Rome.

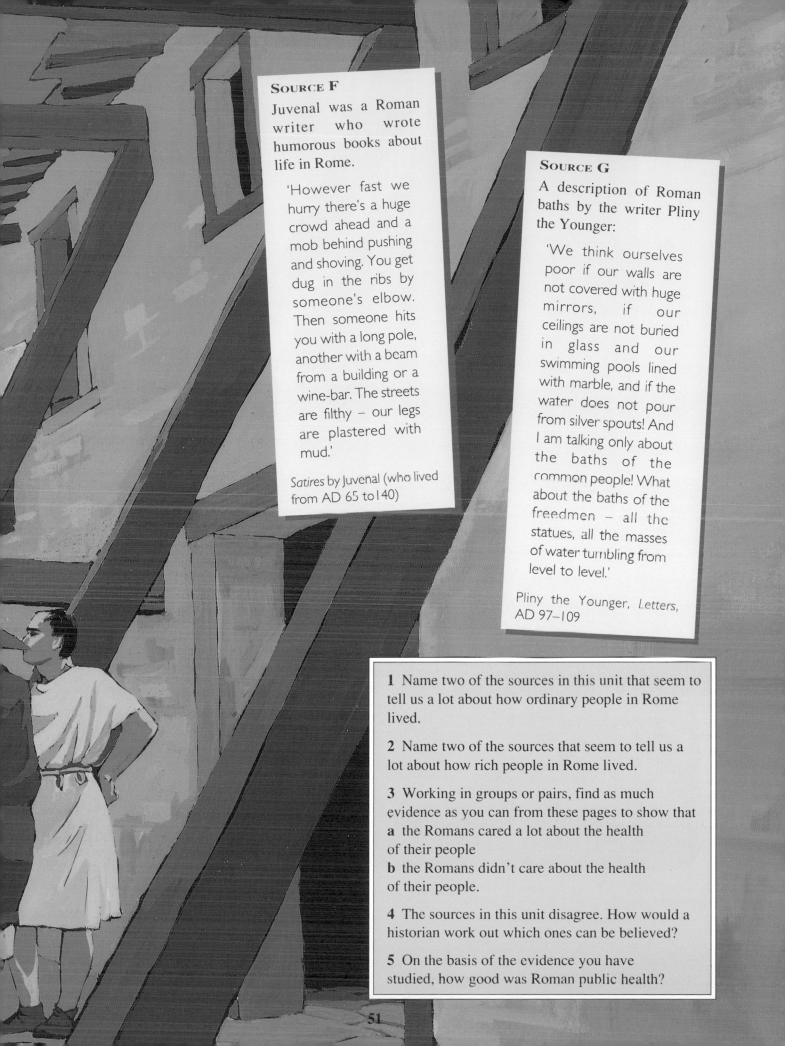

SOURCE F

Juvenal was a Roman writer who wrote humorous books about life in Rome.

'However fast we hurry there's a huge crowd ahead and a mob behind pushing and shoving. You get dug in the ribs by someone's elbow. Then someone hits you with a long pole, another with a beam from a building or a wine-bar. The streets are filthy – our legs are plastered with mud.'

Satires by Juvenal (who lived from AD 65 to 140)

SOURCE G

A description of Roman baths by the writer Pliny the Younger:

'We think ourselves poor if our walls are not covered with huge mirrors, if our ceilings are not buried in glass and our swimming pools lined with marble, and if the water does not pour from silver spouts! And I am talking only about the baths of the common people! What about the baths of the freedmen – all the statues, all the masses of water tumbling from level to level.'

Pliny the Younger, *Letters*, AD 97–109

1 Name two of the sources in this unit that seem to tell us a lot about how ordinary people in Rome lived.

2 Name two of the sources that seem to tell us a lot about how rich people in Rome lived.

3 Working in groups or pairs, find as much evidence as you can from these pages to show that
a the Romans cared a lot about the health of their people
b the Romans didn't care about the health of their people.

4 The sources in this unit disagree. How would a historian work out which ones can be believed?

5 On the basis of the evidence you have studied, how good was Roman public health?

XIV

ROMAN RULE: BLESSING OR CURSE?

We have seen that the Romans traded with the peoples of their empire. They also built great roads and buildings all over the empire. For whose benefit was all this?

Did the Romans take all they could from the people they conquered? Or did the subject peoples gain most from the empire?

SOURCE A

Taxes being collected for the Romans by an official (centre) in Germany. The local men have beards, and wear wool coats. The payment was recorded in the book on the left. The book shows that this relief was carved at the time of the late Roman Empire, but the scene cannot have changed much over the centuries.

You might already have some answers to these questions. Before you investigate further, discuss your views on the Romans so far. Make two lists with examples from what you've found out so far:

- Good things the Romans did.
- Bad things the Romans did.

Now have a look at evidence from different parts of the empire. See who you think the winners and losers were.

SOURCE B

Cicero was a Roman writer and orator. He made many speeches in the Senate. In this speech he explains where Rome's treasures come from.

'Is there one statue, one picture, that has not been captured and brought here from the enemies we have beaten in war? The country houses of our wealthy men are full to overflowing with the countless beautiful things stripped from our most loyal friends.'

Cicero (who lived from 102 to 43 BC)

SOURCE C

Health and hygiene were very important to the Romans. They built public baths in many places in the Roman Empire, often – as here – where there was a natural hot spring. They were used by the Romans and by the local population for washing and relaxation, and as a social meeting place. This bath is part of a complex of baths and buildings at Aquae Sulis ('Waters of the Sun'). We can still see the remains of the baths at Bath today.

53

This speech is supposed to have been made by a British chief, but we think the Roman writer, Tacitus, made up the speech himself. Tacitus had been a governor of Britain. As you read the speech, think about what Tacitus was trying to say about the Romans and the way they ran their empire.

'Our children are now being torn from us to slavery in other lands. Our goods and money are used up in taxes: our land is stripped of its harvest to feed the Romans. Our limbs are aching from building roads through forests and swamps under the whiplash of our oppressors. We Britons are sold into slavery.'

Tacitus, *Agricola*, AD 98

SOURCE E

The aqueduct at Segovia in Spain. The Romans built aqueducts like these in many parts of the empire. They supplied the towns with clean, fresh water. This aqueduct was so well built that it is still in working order.

Aelius Aristides was a Greek who was also a Roman citizen. He wrote about what the Romans did for the peoples of their empire.

'Greek and barbarian can go wherever he likes . . . to be safe it is enough to be a Roman or a subject of Rome . . . You [Rome] have measured the whole world, spanned rivers with bridges, cut through mountains to make level roads for traffic, filled empty places with farms and made life easier by supplying its needs and providing law and order. Everywhere are gymnasia, fountains, gateways, temples, factories and schools. Cities are splendid and the whole earth is as trim as a garden.'

Aelius Aristides, about AD 150

---

1 Read Source F. Explain in your own words the good things the Romans did for the people of the empire.

2 Compare Sources D and F. What differences can you find in the way the Romans treated the peoples of the empire?

3 If Sources D and F disagree, does that mean that one of them must be untrue? Explain your answer.

4 Look through all the sources. What reasons can you think of to explain why people disagree about how well the Romans treated the peoples of the empire?

5 On the basis of all the evidence you have studied, who were the winners and who were the losers in the Roman economic system? Give as much evidence from the sources as you can.

XV

ROMAN GODS AND GODDESSES

> The Roman Empire was vast, and its many and varied people had lots of different beliefs. But the official Roman religion was widely accepted.
>
> **What was the Roman religion like?**

SOURCE A

The Roman religion involved sacrificing animals (killing them and offering them to the gods). Here a bull and a ram are being led to the altar. Later, officials will inspect the entrails (insides). Romans believed that the colour, size and position of the liver, for example, showed whether the gods were pleased or angry.

The official Roman religion

From early times the Romans worshipped many gods and goddesses. They believed that there were spirit gods all around them – in the sea and sky, the mountains and forests. The people honoured these gods and goddesses, who were supposed to bring people good luck.

Rome had many temples, and here the gods were offered sacrifices. Powerful Romans took turns as priests for these temples. The priests were not special holy people; they were often important politicians like Julius Caesar. The priest's job was to take part in ceremonies and ask the gods for things like good weather, big harvests, and protection from enemies. After their death many Roman emperors were believed to become gods. It was the duty of citizens to worship the emperor's statue.

SOME OF THE ROMAN GODS AND GODDESSES	
JUPITER, KING OF THE GODS	APOLLO, GOD OF THE SUN AND YOUTH
JUNO, QUEEN OF THE GODS	CERES, GODDESS OF AGRICULTURE
PLUTO, KING OF THE UNDERWORLD	MARS, GOD OF WAR
NEPTUNE, GOD OF THE SEA	VENUS, GODDESS OF LOVE AND BEAUTY
DIANA, GODDESS OF THE MOON AND HUNTING	BACCHUS, GOD OF WINE

● Can you think of any words in English that come from the names of Roman gods and goddesses?

However, there is evidence that by the time of Augustus, many educated Romans did not take the gods very seriously.

Turning to the stars

Having little faith in the traditional gods, some Romans looked elsewhere for religious ideas. Some, like Lucan in Source B, decided that there were no forces beyond this world. Whether you did well or badly was just a question of luck. Other people came to believe in astrology – the idea that people's lives are shaped by the movement of the stars and the planets.

SOURCE C

This is an extract from a school textbook from Rome.

'My father says you should not believe the astrologers. He says everything happens by accident. I disagree. The patterns of the stars are fixed for all time. God made it that way. The position of the stars determines the future for everyone.'

Anonymous textbook, about AD 100

The mystery religions from the East

Other Romans looked for new exciting religious ideas. They found them in the so-called 'mystery religions' of Greece, Egypt and other parts of the eastern Empire. The 'mystery religions' had their own gods and also had many strange and secret ceremonies to keep believers interested. Unlike the religion of Jupiter and Juno, the 'mystery religions' often promised life after death to believers.

SOURCE D

Both the official Roman religion and the new mystery religions involved sacrifice – killing animals in ceremonies to keep the gods happy. Towards the end of the Roman Empire many people thought that these sacrifices were disgusting and a waste of time.

'They dig a deep pit and put the High Priest in it. Above him they put a loose platform of planks; each plank is drilled with tiny holes. A huge bull is brought onto the platform. They take a sacred hunting spear and plunge it into its heart. Hot blood gushes out of the deep wound. It drains through the holes to fall like rotten rain on the priest in the trench. His clothes and body are covered with the animal's filth. Later he climbs out of the pit. It is horrible to see.'

Prudentius, fourth century AD

● What words in this extract tell you that Prudentius was strongly against animal sacrifices?

A group of Romans meet in a tavern to have a drink of wine. As they drink they start talking about religion.

Working in a small group, produce a script of their conversation. Use evidence from this unit to bring out the fact that Romans had lots of different opinions about religion.

XVI THE RISE OF CHRISTIANITY

Some Romans turned away from the state religion and turned to a new religion, Christianity. In the fourth century AD Christianity became the new official religion, and the worship of the old Roman gods was banned.

Why did Christianity take over?

The official state religion

We have seen that there were a number of different religions in the Roman Empire. One of those was the official government religion. People were expected to worship the Emperor's statue because he was not only the ruler, but also believed to be a god. If you followed the government religion you were, of course, obeying the government.

A dangerous new religion: Christianity

The Romans usually allowed the people they conquered to carry on with their own religions. But the Romans punished or persecuted any people who believed in a religion that was thought dangerous or threatening to the Roman government. One of these 'dangerous' religions was Christianity. What did the Christians believe in?

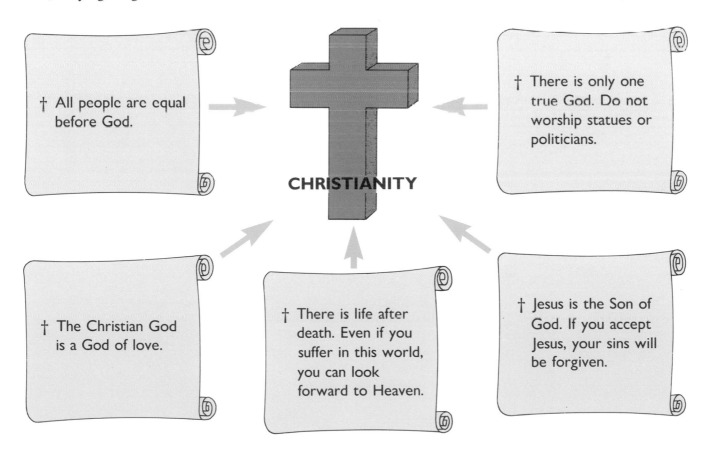

† All people are equal before God.

† There is only one true God. Do not worship statues or politicians.

CHRISTIANITY

† The Christian God is a God of love.

† There is life after death. Even if you suffer in this world, you can look forward to Heaven.

† Jesus is the Son of God. If you accept Jesus, your sins will be forgiven.

Some of the Christian beliefs. Why do you think the Roman emperors were so frightened of this new religion?

The early Christians

Jesus was born during the reign of Augustus in a Roman province, Palestine. Many people were attracted to Jesus' teachings. He preached a new religion. In particular, many poor people took up the new faith. It offered them hope and promised them rewards in Heaven if they followed the Christian teaching.

After Jesus was crucified by the Roman governor, Pontius Pilate, in the first century AD, the followers of Jesus spread the Christian message through Asia, to Greece, and then to Rome.

Early persecution

Many emperors such as Nero and Diocletian tried to stamp out Christianity. Christians were often forced to meet in secret, and worship in underground caves called catacombs.

Even though the Christians were persecuted, the Christian Church kept on growing. As Christianity spread across the Empire, the Church also became more organised. Councils were held to discuss the teachings of the Church and bishops were chosen for all the main cities.

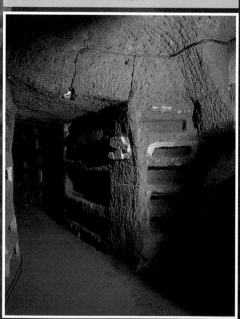

SOURCE A

Inside the underground catacombs in Rome. They are the biggest ones discovered. At the time of a funeral, the early Christians met in secret in one of the tiny underground chapels (large picture). The niches for the bodies were cut lengthwise (left), and sealed with stone slabs.

Constantine: the convert

As hard as they tried, the Roman emperors could not stop the spread of Christianity. The Emperor Constantine realised this. In AD 313 he announced that all religions could be worshipped freely. Christians would no longer be persecuted. Christianity became the official religion of the Empire. On his death bed, Constantine was converted to Christianity and baptised a Christian.

Why did Christianity take over? Can you add any more reasons to this diagram?

1 Explain in your own words how people were attracted to Christianity.

2 'Some people were excited by Christian ideas, others were frightened.' How can you explain these different reactions?

In AD 43 the Romans invaded a new and distant land: Britain became yet another Roman province.

BRITAIN: THE

What the Britons (Celts) did

They enjoyed sports and games, especially fighting.

They worshipped lots of different gods and goddesses who controlled nature. Sucellos, for example, was the sky god of thunder. Druids (priests) performed some religious ceremonies.

Britain was not a united country. The Britons lived in small tribes ruled by chieftains or kings. They built forts on the top of hills for defence.

Most lived in round farmhouses. They grew corn and kept cattle and sheep.

They spoke Celtic. They had no written language, but they did have laws.

'EDGE OF THE WORLD'

The Roman army came in their legions.

They had laws and a written language (Latin).

Good roads were made so that the Roman army could move quickly across the country.

New taxes had to be paid, in money or goods.

There were new entertainments, like gladiator fighting.

Temples and shrines were built to the Roman gods and goddesses, like Jupiter and Mars.

They built stone villas which had workshops and fields.

The Romans brought luxury goods like wine from the Mediterranean, silver goblets and Italian pottery.

Christianity became the official religion from the second century AD.

BRITAIN BEFORE THE ROMANS

> *Before the Romans came to Britain there was no reading and writing in Britain. Our evidence about the Britons comes mainly from archaeological remains. The only written evidence on the Britons comes from Roman writers.*
>
> ***What can we learn about the way the Britons lived?***

The work of Caesar

Julius Caesar was not only a politician and a general, he was also a writer. In 55 BC and 54 BC he brought Roman soldiers to Britain, although he did not actually conquer it. Later he wrote about Britain in his series of books, *The Gallic War*s.

SOURCE A

'The Britons use either bronze or gold coinage. Sometimes instead of coined money they use iron bars of a standard weight. In the interior of the island there is tin to be found, and in coastal areas iron.

The natural shape of the island is triangular and one of the sides lies facing Gaul. One corner of this side is Cantium, where almost all the ships from Gaul come into land. Cantium faces east and the other corner which is lower down points towards the south. This side is about 500 miles long. The second side runs in the direction of Spain and the west, where Hibernia lies. This is an island which is thought to be half the size of Britain and which lies the same distance from Britain as Britain is from Gaul. Halfway across is an island called Mona. There are also thought to be many smaller islands which lie nearer the coast of Britain. The length of this side is 700 miles according to local opinion.

Some writers have suggested that in the middle of winter there is continual night there for thirty whole days. By using a water-clock we noted that the nights were shorter than on the continent.

The third side points northwards and has no land lying opposite it. The corner on that side, however, generally faces Germany. This side is supposed to be 800 miles long, so the whole island is 2,000 miles all the way round.

Of all the Britons, the inhabitants of Cantium, which is on the coast, are by far the most civilised and are very little different from the Gauls in their way of life. Most of those who live inland do not sow grain but live on milk and meat and dress in animal skins. All the Britons, certainly, dye themselves with woad which produces a blue dye and makes them look wild in battle. They wear their hair long and shave every part of their body except the head and upper lip.

Wives are shared by groups of 10 or 12 men, especially by brothers or by fathers and sons, but the children born are reckoned to belong to the first husband the woman takes up with.'

Julius Caesar, *The Gallic Wars*, describing the years 58–52 BC

SOURCE B

A British torque, dated to about 20 BC, found in Norfolk. A torque was a piece of twisted gold or silver jewellery worn round the neck by the Britons. It may have been used to hold a cloak in place, or simply for decoration.

SOURCE C

A British slave chain, found in Wales. It is thought to have been made shortly before the Romans invaded.

Here, actors show how the chains may have been used to control slaves.

Reconstruction of a British pre-Roman farmhouse. It is thought that as many as fifteen to twenty people would live in a farmhouse like this.

SOURCE D

Iron currency bars found in Hampshire. They were used instead of money. Each bar was up to one metre in length.

Other people wrote about Britain too. Strabo was a Greek who wrote about history and geography. His book describes what he knew about the geography of the world as it was known in his day.

SOURCE E

'Most of the island is flat and covered in forests, though there are many hilly areas. Grain, cattle, gold, silver and iron are found on the island. They are exported together with hides, slaves and excellent hunting dogs. The Gauls use these and their own dogs in warfare.

The Britons are taller than the Gauls, their hair is not so yellow and their bodies are more gangling. To give some idea of their size, I saw some of them in Rome, just young boys, but they towered half a foot above the tallest people there. What is more, they were bandy-legged and their bodies all crooked.

Their way of life is a bit like that of the Gauls but much cruder and more barbaric. For example, although they have plenty of milk, some of them do not know how to make cheese, nor do they know anything about keeping gardens or farms. In war they mainly use chariots, just as some of the Gauls do. Their cities are the forests. They cut down the trees and fence in a large round space. In this enclosure they build their huts and corral their cattle but they do not stay in any one place for very long.

They have more rain than snow and on days when there is no rain the fog hangs about for so long that the sun shines for only three or four hours around midday.

Apart from some other small islands around Britain there is a large one called Ierne. About this island I can say nothing definitely except that the inhabitants are fiercer than the Britons and that they are man-eaters.'

Strabo, *Geography*, first century BC

---

1 Use Source A to draw a map of Britain. Your map should show only what Julius Caesar knew about Britain. Put a key on the map – try to include Hibernia, Mona, Cantium, the length of the sides of Britain, and anything else he mentions.
♦ How useful is Caesar's description of Britain for a historian?

2 Here are six statements written by Caesar and Strabo in Sources A and E. Explain whether each statement is shown to be true or false by the archaeological evidence (Sources B, C, D).
♦ Sometimes instead of coined money they use iron bars of a standard weight.
♦ Most of those who live inland dress in animal skins.
♦ Gold, silver and iron are found on the island.
♦ They are exported together with hides, slaves and hunting dogs.
♦ Nor do they know anything about keeping gardens or farms.
♦ They do not stay in any one place for very long.

3 Compare what Caesar and Strabo write about Britain in Sources A and E.
a Which account is more useful to a historian?
b Which account is more reliable?

4 Can we learn more from the archaeological sources or from the written sources?

XVIII

CLAUDIUS:

WHY DID HE INVADE?

In AD 43, Roman legions invaded Britain. They stayed for over 400 years.

Why did Claudius order the invasion of Britain?

Julius Caesar had raided Britain in 55 and 54 BC. Look back at the last unit. Why do you think the Romans might want to conquer Britain?

Who was Claudius?

The emperors who ruled after Julius Caesar got no further than talking about an invasion of Britain. Then in AD 41 the young 'mad' Emperor Caligula was assassinated. Caligula had been responsible for the deaths of members of his own family, as well as huge numbers of ordinary Romans.

Claudius, the uncle of Caligula, became the next Emperor. Claudius stuttered and had a reputation as an old fool, but when he took power he showed that he could run the Empire. His nephew, Caligula, had murdered his wife, his sister and many other Romans. Claudius was keen to bring back law and order.

Claudius orders the invasion

Claudius had been in power for less than two years when he ordered the invasion of Britain. Was this his way of proving he was a successful emperor?

Merchants and generals were keen on the plan because Britain was rich, it produced crops and metals. The Celtic tribes of Britain were weak and divided so would not put up much of a fight. It seemed to Claudius too good an opportunity to miss. So in AD 43 the invasion took place.

The diagram on the next page shows some possible reasons why Emperor Claudius may have launched the invasion. As you look through the following sources, see if you can find any more motives.

Area conquered by Roman army at time of Claudius

AD 43 Roman army landed near Richborough

SOURCE A
Bronze head of Claudius, 'the old fool' who invaded Britain.

Why did Claudius decide to invade Britain?
Which motive do you think was the most important?

Motives for conquering Britain.

A long time ago Julius Caesar showed that the Romans could beat the Britons

War between British chiefs broke out in AD42 and threatened trade with Rome.

SOURCE C

A modern historian made a study of Roman Britain.

'We do not really know why Claudius sent his legions. Perhaps he was after metal ore. He may have wanted a good corn-growing area, or perhaps he thought a free Britain was a nuisance to the Empire. Maybe he only wanted to show that he could capture a country.

Many tribes, including the Iceni, welcomed the Romans or at least surrendered without a fight.'

Ian Andrews, *Boudica Against Rome*, 1972

SOURCE D

Robert Graves was a modern poet and historian. He wrote a historical novel about Claudius. The story-teller is Claudius himself.

'The question of an invasion of Britain was from time to time raised; there was always a good reason for postponing it.

I learned that Togodumnus [then a British chief] and Caractacus [another chief] were about to be involved in a fight with their neighbours, the Iceni, so that trade with Britain would be interrupted if I did not do something. The chance seemed too good to miss.'

Robert Graves, *Claudius the God*, 1934

SOURCE B

Agricola became Governor of Britain, and Tacitus was his son-in-law. His book, *Agricola*, was produced about fifty years after the invasion.

'The climate is wretched, with its rain and mists. The Britons are barbarians, but they show more spirit than the Gauls. Some of them fight from chariots, but their strength is in their infantry. It is rare that two or three tribes join up to drive off a common danger. So, fighting in separate groups, all are conquered.'

Tacitus, *Agricola*, AD 98

---

1 a Read Sources B, C and D, then copy and complete the diagram above, giving more reasons why Claudius conquered Britain. Leave lots of space, because you may find several more motives to add to your diagram.

b Some of the reasons for invading Britain had existed for a long time. Shade them all one colour and show this on a key.

c Some of the reasons were 'short term'. They had become important only a short time before the invasion. Shade them another colour.

2 Source D is from a historical novel.
a What is a historical novel?
b Can we trust historical novels? Does Source D provide evidence of Claudius' motives for invading Britain? Explain your answer.

3 Do you think the Romans were bound to invade Britain?

4 On the basis of all the evidence you have studied, which do you think was the most important reason why Claudius ordered the invasion?

XIX

ROMAN TOWNS IN BRITAIN

The Romans brought town life to Britain. Towns were an important part of the Roman way of living.

What was life like in the towns of Britain?

SOURCE A

Chichester – a town in West Sussex – today. Its Roman name was Noviomagus. Are there any clues in the picture to suggest that this was once a Roman town?

What is a town?

To the Romans, towns were the sign of a civilised country. They were centres for local government, religious and social life. Often built on important routeways, towns were also centres for local merchants, craftsmen and women and farmers to do business.

In Britain, many towns like Deva (Chester) developed out of military bases. Other towns had been the sites of earlier Celtic settlements, like Calleva (Silchester), or were health resorts, like Aquae Arnemetiae (Buxton) or Aquae Sulis (Bath). Roman towns depended upon the countryside around them to provide the food and trade that were needed to survive. They did not contain offices or factories like many towns and cities do today. But there might have been some light industry like metal-working or glass-making in the town.

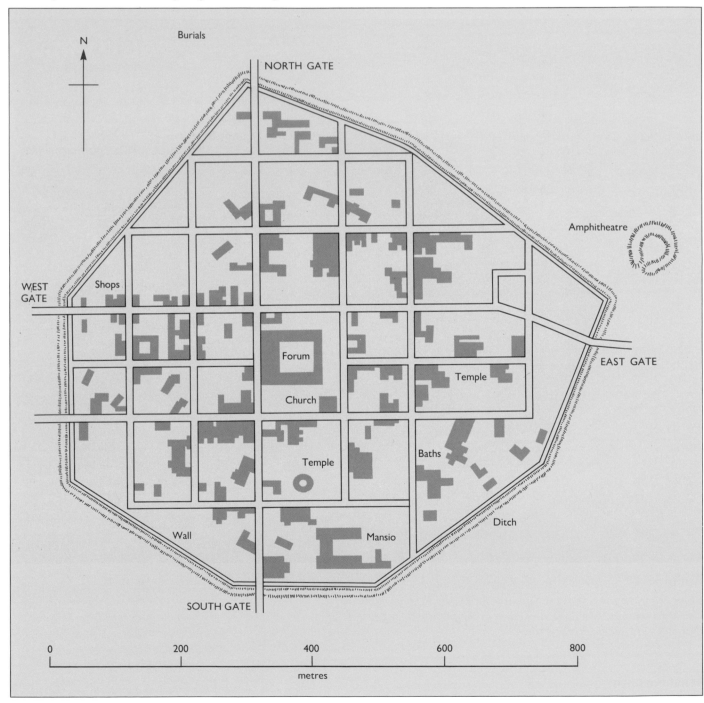

SOURCE B

Silchester in the third century AD. Its Roman name was Calleva.

How do we tell if a place is a town?

The archaeologist John Wacher has said that to work out if a Roman settlement can be called a town or not, you have to look for some sign of the items listed here.

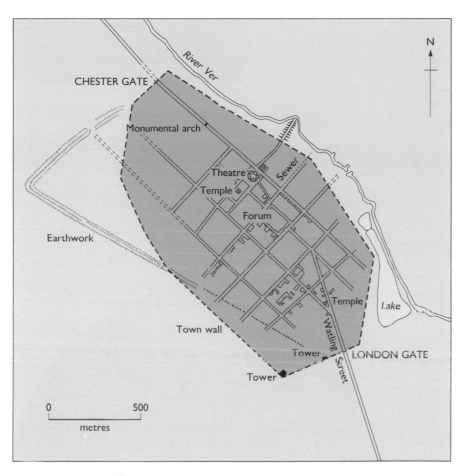

SOURCE C

St Albans in the fourth century AD. Its Roman name was Verulamium.

★ **Trade or industry**
   Shops, a market-place, perhaps some signs of industry like pottery-making.

★ **Local government**
   A forum. This was the market-place. It was usually found right in the middle of a town. People could meet and do business here. A basilica (town hall) was the centre of local government.

★ **Important roads and rivers**
   If a town was an important meeting place it might have a large building called a mansio near one of the gates. This was a kind of hotel for travellers.

★ **Protection and welfare**
   A wall or ditch to keep enemies away. Sewers, drains or baths to keep the people clean and healthy.

★ **Entertainment**
   An amphitheatre, for example.

★ **Town planning**
   Streets were straight and laid out on a grid plan.

● These two maps are drawn to different scales. Which town is larger?

Look at Sources B and C. According to John Wacher, a town should have most if not all of those things that are listed on this page.

Could Silchester and St Albans be called towns? Explain your answers carefully.

CHRISTIANITY IN BRITAIN

XX

Christianity was accepted as the official religion in the Roman Empire in AD 313. But did this mean everybody in the Empire became a Christian straight away? Or did some people still worship their old gods?

How can we find out about the spread of Christian ideas in Roman Britain?

Look at the following sources and try to work out how Christian Roman Britain was. Sources A and B were written by historians in the third century AD. Neither of them had actually visited Britain.

SOURCE A

The Christian historian Tertullian wrote that there were:

'places in Britain unknown to the Romans, but which have submitted to Christ.'

Tertullian, *Against the Jews*, AD 200

SOURCE B

The Christian historian Origen wrote:

'The Christian religion acted as a unifying force even in the land of Britain.'

Origen, AD 240

SOURCE C

In AD 314 there was a meeting in Gaul of Christian bishops from all over the Roman Empire. Amongst them were:

'Eborius, bishop of the city of York in the province of Britain; Restitutus, bishop of the city of London; Adelphius, bishop of the city of Lincoln.'

Acts of the Council of Arles, AD 314

A very important clue we have is the shape ☧. This is called the chi-rho symbol, and it stood for the first two letters of the Greek word for 'Christ'. When we find this symbol we know that there must have been some Christians living, working and worshipping in the area.

SOURCE D

Part of a mosaic floor at Hinton St Mary, Dorset. It was probably made in about AD 335–355.

A reconstruction of a wall painting from about AD 350. Lullingstone Roman villa, Kent.

SOURCE E

The modern archaeologist Mortimer Wheeler wrote about a famous Iron Age hillfort in Dorset, called Maiden Castle.

'About AD 380, part of the old fortress became a temple. A bronze plaque [plate] from the site bears a figure of Minerva [a Roman goddess]; a small bronze three-horned bull-god, found elsewhere in Britain . . . a fragment of a marble statue showing Diana [a Roman goddess], and a Mars-like god might also have been present.'

Mortimer Wheeler, *Maiden Castle*, 1972

SOURCE F

'To [the god] Jupiter, Greatest and best, perfection. Lucius Septimus, Governor of Britannia Prima, and a citizen of Reims, restored this.'

Inscription in stone from Cirencester, Gloucestershire, about AD 314

SOURCE G

Part of some treasure found at Water Newton in Cambridgeshire. Here there are three vessels, three plaques and a wine strainer made of silver. There are 28 objects altogether. About AD 325.

---

1 Which sources suggest that there were Christians in Britain before AD 313?

2 Which sources suggest that Christianity was not the only religion in Britain after AD 313?

3 'Most people in Britain were Christians after AD 313.' Do you think this statement is 'true' or 'false'? Explain your answer carefully.

XXI

EMPIRE IN DANGER

For about two centuries after the reign of Emperor Augustus, the Roman Empire was strong and peaceful. Roman wealth and civilisation spread to all the provinces. But from about AD 200, the Empire started to weaken. The first cracks began to appear.

Why did the Empire start to decline?

The barbarians invade

A big problem for the Romans were the frequent attacks from barbarians. The barbarians were a mixture of tribes such as Goths, Vandals, Franks and Saxons, and they lived in small farming settlements north of the River Danube. Although the Romans called them barbarians, they were not just wild savages: the Romans used the word 'barbarian' for any foreigner living outside the Empire.

The barbarian tribes were looking for new land further south, inside the frontiers of the Roman Empire, where the climate was milder. The Romans found it harder and harder to stop the barbarians. They could no longer defend their long frontiers. Finally they allowed some of the tribes to settle inside the Empire.

At the end of the fourth century a new barbarian enemy appeared. A tribe called the Huns moved from central Asia to northern Europe, looking for new land. In AD 376, about 10,000 Goths flooded into the Roman Empire to escape from the Huns. The Roman frontier collapsed. Thousands of Goths then marched south and in 410 reached the gates of Rome. For two days they ransacked the great city.

A divided empire

The Emperor Diocletian ruled from 284 to 305. He was strong and powerful, but even he realised that it was no longer possible for one person to control such a vast empire. He ruled from the East, and a soldier called Maximian looked after the West.

In 395 the Roman Empire finally broke into two separate pieces, each with its own emperor. The East was ruled from Constantinople. The West was ruled from Rome. Within a century, the Western Empire had collapsed. The Eastern Empire continued until the collapse of Constantinople in 1453.

The army gets weaker

The army grew in size towards the end of the Empire as more and more soldiers were needed to defend the long Roman frontier. But the army was becoming weaker.

Barbarian warriors were allowed to join the Roman army. They often fought well for the Empire, and sometimes made up as much as 60 per cent of the Roman forces in a battle. But there were fewer Romans in the army at a time when there were more barbarian attacks on the borders of the Empire.

Many Romans had grown used to peace: the empire was no longer expanding. Some Roman soldiers did not really want to fight.

Who will pay?

High taxes were needed to pay for extra soldiers to protect the frontiers. Unfortunately this came at a time when the population was declining. There were more taxes to pay, but fewer people to pay them. The rich people did not pay taxes, so the burden fell on the poor. This caused lots of problems. Some poor people refused to pay taxes. Others fought against the Empire and took part in revolts.

Weak and selfish emperors

Perhaps if the emperors had been stronger, the Empire could have been saved. Between AD 96 and 180 there were five strong emperors who ruled the Empire well. But later on, with no fixed way of choosing the next emperor, there was nothing to stop selfish men from fighting for power. Successful generals often fought their way to power with their soldiers, and killed the ruling emperor. For example, between AD 211 and 284 there were 23 emperors, and 20 of them were murdered. Often they were more interested in getting rich and living a life of luxury, than ruling the Empire properly.

The Barbarians invade

A divided empire
Constantinople
Rome
Western Empire
Eastern Empire

The army gets weaker

Who will pay?
Lots
Taxes
Population
None

Weak and selfish emperors

1 Show on a timeline some of the problems that the Roman Empire faced between AD 200 and 450.

2 You read in a book that 'the Roman Empire fell apart because of attacks from barbarians'.
a Explain in your own words who the barbarians were.
b Do you think that the problems of the Empire can all be blamed on the barbarians?

3 Work in a small group. You are in charge of the Roman Empire. The year is AD 350. Decide what you would do to stop the collapse of the Empire.

XXII

DECLINE AND FALL

The Roman Empire in the West came to an end in the fifth century AD when Rome was over-run by barbarians. In the last unit we looked at some possible causes for the decline of Rome.

For centuries, historians have disagreed about the causes. What different explanations have historians produced?

Let us look at the ideas of two very different historians, Edward Gibbon and Moses Finley.

Edward Gibbon is one of the best-known historians of the Roman Empire. The first volume of his huge book, *The Decline and Fall of the Roman Empire*, appeared in 1776 and was a best-seller. The book is six volumes long and looks at the history of Rome from the first century AD to the collapse of the Eastern Empire in 1453. Modern historians think that Gibbon's research was careful and usually accurate.

Gibbon was a rich gentleman and he travelled widely in Europe. Like many educated people in the eighteenth century, he had read many books on ancient Greece and Rome. He wanted to explain both how and why the Empire fell.

Gibbon lived at a time when religion was very important to people, and when the Church was very powerful. When Gibbon said that Christianity might have helped cause the fall of the Roman Empire, he was criticised by many people.

SOURCE A

Gibbon did not think there was only a single cause for the fall of the Empire. But he put forward an important new cause which was not popular: Christianity.

This is a list of some of the reasons Gibbon gives for why the Roman Empire fell.

'1 Barbarian tribes repeatedly attacked the Empire.

2 Many emperors were weak and bad at ruling.

3 The sheer size of the Empire was a problem.

4 Christianity caused arguments and weakened the Empire.'

Edward Gibbon, *The Decline and Fall of the Roman Empire*, 1776

According to Gibbon, Christianity caused arguments and weakness within the Roman Empire.

1 a What does Source A say caused the downfall of the Roman Empire?
b What does Source B say caused the downfall of the Roman Empire?
c Does Source A agree or disagree with Source B? Explain your answer carefully.

2 Is this sentence 'true' or 'false': 'Source B was written later than Source A, so it must be better'?

3 Look back at the rest of this book. What other reasons do you think caused the Roman Empire to fall? Explain your answer carefully.

4 Why do you think there are many different explanations for the collapse of the Roman Empire in the West?

5 'Things always get better.' Using the example of the Roman Empire, explain whether you agree or disagree with this statement.

SOURCE B

This has been adapted from a well-known book by a twentieth-century historian, Moses Finley. Like many recent historians, he thought that economic causes were very important in explaining the decline and fall.

'The Roman Empire could not change. The army could not be made bigger because men were needed to work on farms.
    Farming was harder because of high taxes. Taxes were high because the army needed more money to pay the soldiers. The army could not be made bigger because . . . '

M. I. Finley, *Aspects of Antiquity*, 1960

This diagram shows the ideas of Moses Finley.

XXIII

THE LEGACY OF ROME

It is nearly 2,000 years since the Roman Empire was at its most powerful.
Even though the Roman world ended long ago, it still has an impact on the way we live today.

What aspects of Roman life still affect us in the modern world?

SOURCE A

The theatre at Ephesus, in modern Turkey. It was built by the Romans in the first century AD.

An enduring impact

The Romans left their mark all over their Empire. In Britain many roads still follow the routes laid out by the Roman engineers. Some towns, like London, Exeter, York and Chester, continue to be as important today as they were when the Romans founded them. Other towns, like Wroxeter in Shropshire, fell into disuse after the Romans left, but remain for modern archaeologists to investigate. Spectacular Roman remains can still be seen in much of Europe, the Middle East and North Africa.

The classical tradition

Roman ideas have had a long life. The Roman way of building continues to influence architecture today. Roman styles were popular among many European architects between 1500 and 1900. Famous buildings like St Paul's Cathedral in London, and the White House in Washington, USA, follow Roman models.

Catholics and the Roman connection

The Catholic Church is a direct link between the modern world and the Roman Empire. Its headquarters were set up in Rome in the days of the Empire. The leader of the Church, the Pope, calls himself 'Pontifex Maximus'. This is the traditional title for the chief priest of the Roman Empire. Latin is still the official language of the Catholic Church. As recently as the 1960s, all Catholic church services were held in Latin.

SOURCE B

A Roman road today. This one leads out of Lincoln (which in Roman times was called 'Lindum'). It follows the original route built by the Romans in the first century AD.

The Romans built a network of first-class roads across the Empire. Roman roads were often raised on an embankment above the countryside they passed through. This is why these roads later became known as 'highways'.

77

Latin and the way we speak today

Let us look in a little more detail at one particular way in which the Romans have had a big impact on modern life: language. The Latin language was spoken all over the Empire. Latin has had a huge influence on many European languages spoken today.

After the collapse of the Empire, people in many parts of the Empire continued to speak Latin. As time passed, the Latin of different areas began to change, until a series of new languages emerged. These Latin-based languages include modern Italian, Spanish, French, Portuguese and Romanian.

Look at the table below and you will see how similar all these languages are to each other and to Latin.

English – a 'magpie' language

English is a very mixed language. When the Romans invaded Britain in the first century AD, they brought Latin with them. Many Latin words entered the Celtic language which the Britons spoke at that time.

When the Anglo-Saxons invaded Britain from Germany and Denmark in the fifth century, they spoke a language known as Anglo-Saxon (or Old English). Anglo-Saxon became the main language spoken in Britain.

Later, in 1066, the Normans conquered Britain. The Normans spoke French, which was full of Latin words, so more Latin words poured into the English language. So in various ways, the English language has borrowed widely from Latin over the centuries.

English is a very rich language. Look at these three columns of words of similar meaning. The first consists of words descended from Old English (Anglo-Saxon), the second of words from Latin through French, and the third of words taken directly from Latin.

From Old English	From Latin (via French)	From Latin
fast	firm	secure
fire	flame	conflagration
fear	terror	trepidation
holy	sacred	consecrated

1 Many towns in Britain nowadays have names that end with -chester, -caster or -cester. This comes from the Latin word 'castrum', meaning an army camp. It tells us that the town was probably a Roman settlement.
Work as a pair. Using an atlas, find as many of these place-names as you can.

2 Use a good dictionary that explains where words come from. Can you find ten modern English words that come from Latin?

3 Look at all the information in this unit. Which contribution of the Romans to the modern world is, in your opinion, the most important?

The numbers 1 to 10 in some Latin-based languages.

	Latin	Italian	Spanish	French	Portuguese	Romanian
1	unus	uno	uno	un	um	un
2	duo	due	dos	deux	dois	doi
3	tres	tre	tres	trois	três	trei
4	quattuor	quattro	cuatro	quatre	quarto	patru
5	quinque	cinque	cinco	cinq	cinco	cinci
6	sex	sei	seis	six	seis	şase
7	septem	sette	siete	sept	sete	şapte
8	octo	otto	ocho	huit	oito	opt
9	novem	nove	nueve	neuf	nove	noua
10	decem	dieci	diez	dix	dez	zece

INDEX